FIRST EI

LIVING ON THE EDGE

TEXAS

DURING THE CIVIL WAR AND RECONSTRUCTION

Edited by Patrick J. Kelly and Rhonda Minten
The University of Texas at San Antonio

Bassim Hamadeh, CEO and Publisher
Michael Simpson, Vice President of Acquisitions
Jamie Giganti, Senior Managing Editor
Miguel Macias, Graphic Designer
David Miano, Specialist Acquisitions Editor
Monika Dziamka, Project Editor
Brian Fahey, Licensing Specialist
Claire Yee, Interior Designer

First published in the United States of America in 2016 by Cognella, Inc.

Printed in the United States of America

ISBN: 978-1-62661-053-8 (pbk) / 978-1-62661-054-5 (br)

www.cognella.com 800-200-3908

Contents

Dedication

I dedicate this book to my co-author, Rhonda Minten. This project was Rhonda's idea, and her enthusiasm, hard work, and belief in the importance of primary evidence for the teaching of history saw it through to completion.

—Patrick Kelly

This book is dedicated to Emily Khalil, my daughter, and Patrick Kelly, my co-author and mentor, both of whom inspire me every day.

—Rhonda Minten

Introduction

The Civil War era became a defining moment for Texas. In the years leading up to the American Civil War, Texas possessed a unique set of characteristics that drew it into and pushed it further away from the heart of the Confederacy. After decades of dynamic uncertainty, one border of Texas sat on the precipice of America's Western frontier, another lay precariously between the United States and Mexico, and yet another bordered and embraced the deep-rooted slave culture of the American South. Texans reflected each of these diverse cultures, and events in Texas introduced a distinct perspective to the upcoming domestic hostilities.

Reconstruction and reorganization following the Civil War brought further exceptional challenges for Texans. Because Texas bordered at the edge of the Confederacy, few battles and relatively little property destruction occurred within the state; however, dramatic economic, political, and social change contributed to the upheaval and turmoil that rocked Texas throughout the late 1860s and 1870s. Newly-freed slaves struggled to find stability and acceptance, while Anglos fought to retain social and economic dominance. In addition, Texans continued to experience the ordeals of the Western frontier. Many areas were isolated, lonely, and lawless. Indian attacks were common, and the environment was rugged. Settlers endured extraordinary circumstances in order to create new communities—often at the expense of long-established Native American communities in the area.

In Texas, the tenuous relationship between Anglos, Tejanos, Native Americans, and African Americans evolved to trigger new animosities but also created new alliances. The intermingling of cultures within Texas brought challenges and opportunities that were reflected in contemporary accounts. They write about their attempts to construct their lives, perpetuate their heritage, and institute boundaries while establishing civilization. The primary documents provide a map across social classes, geographic areas, and diverse ethnicities. The documents record the exceptional and mundane events of everyday life during a dramatic and fascinating era. These firsthand accounts give insight into the uncertainties and ambitions that motivated those who attempted to define Texas during the Civil War and Reconstruction.

Reading and Understanding Primary Documents

[1]What factors establish the value of a primary source? To understand a primary document, readers first must establish who created the source. Find out details about the author and other participants. Determine when and why the document was created and what circumstances influenced its creation. What information does it contain? What information is left out? Who was the intended audience? What additional information can you examine that refer to the events addressed in the document? Does the document confirm or contest the information contained in other sources? What questions does the document raise about the events and the people who recorded them? What factors influenced the perceptions of the people involved? Most importantly, what does the document reveal about history? What did people choose to record and relate, why did people behave as they did, and what were the consequences?

1 Kathryn Walbert, "Reading Primary Sources: An Introduction for Students," adapted by Patrick Kelly and Rhonda Minten.

Primary Source Analysis

Identify the source

1. What is the nature of the source?
2. Who created this source, and what do I know about him or her?
3. When was the source produced?
4. Where was the source produced?

Contextualize the source

1. What do you know about the historical context for this source?
2. What do you know about how the CREATOR of this source fits into that historical context?
3. Why did the person create the source?

Explore the source

1. What factual information is conveyed in the source?
2. What opinions are related in this source?
3. What is implied or conveyed unintentionally in the source?
4. What is not said in this source?
5. What is surprising or interesting about this source?
6. What do I not understand in this source?
7. How is this source different from my world?

Evaluate the source

1. How does this source compare to secondary accounts (if any are available)?
2. What do you believe or disbelieve about this source?
3. What do you still not know—and how can you find more information?

1 Giving Voice to the Voiceless—Slave Narratives

Between 1936 and 1938, members of the Federal Writers' Project (part of the WPA) traveled across the United States and interviewed over 2,000 former slaves. These first-hand accounts gave voice to those who had seldom spoken to a receptive audience. Their stories often revealed a pragmatic attitude toward their former lives. Forced servitude was an established circumstance, and the men and women fashioned their lives within the perimeters of slavery. With emancipation, they were compelled to adapt to confusing new boundaries that were often daunting. The following narratives offer insight into the diverse experiences of Will Adams, Sarah Ashley, William Branch, and Katie Darling, slaves who lived in Texas during the Civil War and Reconstruction. As you are reading the narratives, think about those who conducted the interviews and the questions they posed to the participants. What questions might they have chosen to elicit particular responses from the participants?

Questions

1. What were the ages of the men and women during the Civil War and Reconstruction? How might their ages at that time influence their perceptions of the events? How might their ages at the time of the interviews change their perceptions of prior events? What other factors might influence their perceptions of the past?

2. Will Adams mentioned the Ku Klux Klan. Whom did he blame for Klan activities during Reconstruction? What factors would influence his opinion on this subject?
3. Sarah Ashley related her experiences as a slave separated from her family. What were some of the rules and regulations she endured? How would you describe her perspective when describing the past?
4. William Branch provided vivid descriptions of his life as a slave and later as an Indian scout for the U.S. Army. What do his recollections of everyday life reveal about his daily routine as a slave? What was his attitude toward his master? How did his life change after the Civil War? What were his experiences as a scout? What was his attitude toward the Indians he encountered? Did he seem satisfied with his life? Explain.
5. Katie Darling nursed seven white children in what she termed the "bullwhip days." Did this term describe the treatment she witnessed and experienced? Explain. What were some of the rituals and daily routines that Katie recalled? How did Katie's master and his wife react to the ending of slavery?
6. What factors about their lives as slaves do the former slaves recall most often?
7. Why did some slaves stay with their former owners following the Civil War?
8. How did their lives change following the Civil War?

Narrative 1

Will Adams (born in 1857)[1]

"My folks allus belongs to the Cavins and wore their name till after 'mancipation. Pa and ma was named Freeman and Amelia Cavin and Massa Dave fotches them to Texas from Alabama, along with ma's mother, what we called Maria.

1 William M. Adams, from *Slave Narratives: A Folk History of Slavery in the United States From Interviews*, vol. XVI, pp. 4-9. Copyright in the Public Domain.

"The Cavins allus thunk lots of their niggers and Grandma Maria say, 'Why shouldn't they—it was their money.' She say there was plenty Indians here when they settled this country and they bought and traded with them without killin' them, if they could. The Indians was poor folks, jus' pilfer and loaf 'round all the time. The niggers was a heap sight better off than they was, 'cause we had plenty to eat and a place to stay.

"Young Massa Tom was my special massa and he still lives here. Old Man Dave seemed to think more of his niggers than anybody and we thunk lots of our white folks. My pa was leader on the farm, and there wasn't no overseer or driver. When pa whip a nigger he needn't go to Massa Dave, but pa say, 'Go you way, you nigger. Freeman didn't whip you for nothin'.' Massa Dave allus believe pa, 'cause he tells the truth.

"One time a peddler come to our house and after supper he goes to see 'bout his pony. Pa done feed that pony fifteen ears of corn. The peddler tell massa his pony ain't been fed nothin', and massa git mad and say, 'Be on you way iffen you gwine 'cuse my niggers of lyin'.'

"We had good quarters and plenty to eat. I 'members when I's jus' walkin' round good pa come in from the field at night and taken me out of bed and dress me and feed me and then play with me for hours. Him bein' leader, he's gone from 'fore day till after night. The old heads got out early but us young scraps slep' till eight or nine o'clock, and don't you think Massa Dave ain't comin' round to see we is fed. I 'members him like it was yest'day, comin' to the quarters with his stick and askin' us, 'Had your breakfas'?' We'd say, 'Yes, suh.' Then he'd ask if we had 'nough or wanted any more. It look like he taken a pleasure in seein' us eat. At dinner, when the field hands come in, it am the same way. He was sho' that potlicker was fill as long as the niggers want to eat.

"The hands worked from sun to sun. Massa give them li'l crops and let them work them on Saturday. Then he bought the stuff and the niggers go to Jefferson and buy clothes and sech like. Lots saved money and bought freedom 'fore the war was over.

"We went to church and first the white preacher preached and then he larns our cullud preachers. I seed him ordain a cullud preacher and he told him to allus be honest. When the white preacher laid his hand on him, all the niggers git to hollerin' and shoutin' and prayin' and that nigger git scart mos' to death.

"On Christmas we had all we could eat and drink and after that a big party, and you ought to see them gals swingin' they partners round. Then massa have two niggers wrestle, and our sports and dances was big sport for the white folks. They'd sit on the gallery and watch the niggers put it on brown.

"Massa didn't like his niggers to marry off the place, but sometimes they'd do it, and massa tell his neighbor, 'My nigger am comin' to you place. Make him behave.' All the niggers 'haved then and they wasn't no Huntsville and gallows and burnin's then.

"Old massa went to war with his boy, Billie. They's lots of cryin' and weepin' when they sot us free. Lots of them didn't want to be free, 'cause they knowed nothin' and had nowhere to go. Them what had good massas stayed right on.

"I 'members when that Ku Klux business starts up. Smart niggers causes that. The carpet-baggers ruint the niggers and the white men couldn't do a thing with them, so they got up the Ku Klux and stirs up the world. Them carpet-baggers come round larnin' niggers to sass the white folks what done fed them. They come to pa with that talk and he told them, 'Listen, white folks, you is gwine start a graveyard if you come round here teachin' niggers to sass white folks." Them carpet-baggers starts all the trouble at 'lections in Reconstruction. Niggers didn't know anythin' 'bout politics.

"Mos' the young niggers ain't usin' the education they got now. I's been here eighty years and still has to be showed and told by white folks. These young niggers won't git told by whites or blacks either. They thinks they done knowed it all and that gits them in trouble.

"I stays with the Cavins mos' twenty years after the war. After I leaves, I allus farms and does odd jobs round town here. I's father of ten chillen by one woman. I lives by myself now and they gives me $13.00 a month. I'd be proud to git it if it wasn't more'n a dollar, 'cause they ain't nothin' a old man can do no more.

Sarah Ashley (born between 1843 and 1845—93 at the time of the interview)[2]

"I ain't able to do nothin' no more. I's jus' plumb give out and I stays here by myself. My daughter, Georgia Grime, she used to live with me but she's been dead four year.

"I was born in Miss'ippi and Massa Henry Thomas buy us and bring us here. He a spec'lator and buys up lots of niggers and sells 'em. Us family was sep'rated. My two sisters and my papa was sold to a man in Georgia. Den dey put me on a block and bid me off. Dat in New Orleans and I scairt and cry, but dey put me up dere anyway. First dey takes me to Georgia and dey didn't sell me for a long spell. Massa Thomas he travel round and buy and sell niggers. Us stay in de spec'lators drove de long time.

"After 'while Massa Mose Davis come from Cold Spring, in Texas, and buys us. He was buyin' up little chillen for he chillen. Dat 'bout four year befo' da first war. I was 19 year old when de burst of freedom come in June and I git turn loose.

"I was workin' in de field den. Jus' befo' dat de old Massa he go off and buy more niggers. He go east. He on a boat what git stove up and he die and never come back no more. Us never see him no more.

"I used to have to pick cotton and sometime I pick 300 pound and tote it a mile to de cotton house. Some pick 300 to 800 pound cotton and have to tote de bag de whole mile to de gin. Iffen dey didn't do dey work dey git whip till dey have blister on 'em. Den iffen dey didn't do it, de man on a hoss goes down de rows and whip with a paddle make with holes in it and bus' de blisters. I never git whip, 'cause I allus git my 300 pound. Us have to go early to do dat, when de horn goes early, befo' daylight. Us have to take de victuals in de bucket to de field.

"Massa have de log house and us live in little houses, strowed in long rows. Dere wasn't no meetin's 'lowed in de quarters and iffen dey have prayer meetin' de boss man whip dem. Sometime us run off at night and

2 Sarah Ashley, from *Slave Narratives: A Folk History of Slavery in the United States From Interviews*, vol. XVI, pp. 34-37. Copyright in the Public Domain.

go to camp meetin'. I takes de white chillen to church sometime, but dey couldn't larn me to sing no songs 'cause I didn' have no spirit.

"Us never got 'nough to eat, so us keeps stealin' stuff. Us has to. Dey give us de peck of meal to last de week and two, three pound bacon in chunk. Us never have flour or sugar, jus' cornmeal and de meat and 'taters. De niggers has de big box under de fireplace, where dey kep' all de pig and chickens what dey steal, down in salt.

"I seed a man run away and de white men got de dogs and dey kotch him and put him in de front room and he jump through de big window and break de glass all up. Dey sho' whips him when dey kotches him.

"De way dey whip de niggers was to strip 'em off naked and whip 'em till dey make blisters and bus' de blisters. Den dey take de saltand red pepper and put in de wounds. After dey wash and grease dem and put somethin' on dem, to keep dem from bleed to death.

"When de boss man told us freedom was come he didn't like it, but he give all us de bale of cotton and some corn. He ask us to stay and he'p with de crop but we'uns so glad to git 'way dat nobody stays. I got 'bout fifty dollars for de cotton and den I lends it to a nigger what never pays me back yit. Den I got no place to go, so I cooks for a white man name' Dick Cole. He sposen give me $5.00 de month but he never paid me no money. He'd give me eats and clothes, 'cause he has de little store.

"Now, I's all alone and thinks of dem old times what was so bad, and I's ready for de Lawd to call me."

Narrative 3

William Branch (born in 1850)[3]

"Yahsur, I was a slave. I was bo'n May 13, 1850, on the place of Lawyer Woodson in Lunenburg County, Virginia. It was 'bout 75 miles southwest of Richmond. They was two big plantations, one on one side the road, yother the yother. My marster owned 75 slaves. He raised tobacco and cotton. I wukked tobacco sometime, sometime cotton. Dere wasn't no whippin' or switchin'. We had to wuk hard. Marster Woodson was a

3 William Branch, from *Slave Narratives: A Folk History of Slavery in the United States From Interviews*, vol. XVI, pp. 143-147. Copyright in the Public Domain.

rich man. He live in a great big house, a lumber house painted white. And it had a great big garden.

"De slaves lives in a long string of log houses. Dey had dirt floors and shingle roofs. Marster Woodson's house was shingle roof too. We had home cured bacon and veg'tables, dried co'n, string beans and dey give us hoe cakes baked in hot ashes. Dere always was lots of fresh milk.

"How'd us slaves git de clothes? We carded de cotton, den de women spin it on a spinnin' wheel. After dat day sew de gahment togeddah on a sewin' machine. Yahsur, we's got sewin' machine, wid a big wheel and a handle. One woman tu'n de handle and de yuther woman do de sewin'.

"Dat's how we git de clothes for de 75 slaves. Marster's clothes? We makes dem for de whole fam'ly. De missis send de pattren and de slaves makes de clothes. Over nigh Richmond a fren' of Marster Woodson has 300 slaves. Dey makes all de clothes for dem.

"I was with Marster twel de Yankees come down to Virginia in 1861. De sergeant of de Yankees takes me up on his hoss and I goes to Washington wid de Yankees. I got to stay dere 'cause I'd run away from my marster.

"I stay at de house of Marse Frank Cayler. He's an ole time hack driver. I was his houseboy. I stay dere twel de year 1870, den I goes to Baltimore and jines de United States Army. We's sent to Texas 'count of de Indians bein' so bad. Dey put us on a boat at Baltimore and we landed at Galveston.

"Den we marches from Galveston to Fort Duncan. It was up, up, de whole time. We ties our bedclothes and rolls dem in a bundle wid a strap. We walks wid our guns and bedclothes on our backs, and de wagons wid de rations follows us. Dey is pulled by mules. We goes 15 miles ev'ry day. We got no tents, night come, we unrolls de blankets and sleeps under de trees, sometime under de brush.

"For rations we got canned beans, milk and hardtack. De hard tacks is 3 or 4 in a box, we wets 'em in water and cooks 'em in a skillet. We gits meat purty often. When we camps for de night de captain say, 'You'all kin go huntin'.' Before we git to de mountains dere's deer and rabbits and dey ain't no fences. Often in de dark we sees a big animal and we shoots. When we bring 'im to camp, de captain say, 'Iffen de cow got iron burns de rancher gwineter shoot hisself a nigger scout.' But de cow ain't got no iron, it's—what de name of de cow what ain't feel de iron?

Mavrick, yahsur. We eats lots[Pg 145] of dem Mavricks. We's goin' 'long de river bottom, and before we comes to Fort Duncan we sees de cactus and muskeet. Dere ain't much cattle, but one colored scout shoots hisself a bear. Den we eats high. Fort Duncan were made of slab lumber and de roof was gravel and grass.

"Den we's ordered to Fort Davis and we's in de mountains now. Climb, climb all day, and de Indians give us a fit ev'ry day. We kills some Indians, dey kills a few soldiers. We was at Fort Clark a while. At Fort Davis I jines de colored Indian Scouts, I was in Capt. George L. Andrew's Co. K.

"We's told de northern Cheyennes is on a rampus and we's goin' to Fort Sill in Indian Territory. Before we gits to Fort Concho (San Angelo) de Comanches and de Apaches give us a fit. We fitten' 'em all de time and when we gits away from de Comanches and Apaches we fitten de Cheyennes. Dey's seven feet tall. Dey couldn't come through that door.

"When we gits to Fort Sill, Gen. Davidson say de Cheyennes is off de reservation, and he say, 'You boys is got to git dem back. Iffen you kill 'em, dey can't git back to de reservation.' Den we goes scoutin' for de Cheyennes and dey is scoutin' for us. Dey gits us first, on de Wichita River was 500 of 'em, and we got 75 colored Indian Scouts. Den Red Foot, de Chief of de Cheyennes, he come to see Capt. Lawson and say he want rations for his Indians. De captain say he cain't give no rations to Indians off de reservation. Red Foot say he don't care 'bout no reservation and he say he take what we got. Capt. Lawson 'low we gotter git reinforcements. We got a guide in de scout troop, he call hisself Jack Kilmartin. De captain say, 'Jack, I'se in trouble, how kin I git a dispatch to Gen. Davidson?' Jack say, 'I kin git it through.' And Jack, he crawl on his belly and through de brush and he lead a pony, and when he gits[Pg 146] clear he rides de pony bareback twel he git to Fort Sill. Den Gen. Davidson, he soun' de gin'ral alarm and he send two companies of cavalry to reinforce us. But de Cheyennes give 'em a fit all de way, dey's gotter cut dere way through de Cheyennes.

"And Col. Shafter comes up, and goes out in de hills in his shirt sleeves jus' like you's sittin' dere. Dey's snow on de groun' and de wind's cole, but de colonel don't care, and he say, 'Whut's dis order Gen. Davidson give? Don' kill de Cheyennes? You kill 'em all from de cradle to de Cross.'

"And den we starts de attack. De Cheyennes got Winchesters and rifles and repeaters from de government. Yahsur, de government give 'em de guns dey used to shoot us. We got de ole fashion muzzle loaders. You puts one ball in de muzzle and shove de powder down wid de ramrod. Den we went in and fit 'em, and 'twas like fightin' a wasp's nest. Dey kills a lot of our boys and we nearly wipes 'em out. Den we disarms de Cheyennes we captures, and turns dere guns in to de regiment.

"I come to San Antonio after I'se mustered out and goes to work for de Bell Jewelry Company and stays dere twel I cain't work no more. Did I like de army? Yahsur, I'd ruthuh be in de army dan a plantation slave."

Katie Darling (born in 1849—about 88 at the time of the interview)[4]

"You is talkin' now to a nigger what nussed seven white chillen in them bullwhip days. Miss Stella, my young missy, got all our ages down in she Bible, and it say I's born in 1849. Massa Bill McCarty my massa and he live east and south of Marshall, clost to the Louisiana line. Me and my three brudders, Peter and Adam and Willie, all lives to be growed and married, but mammy die in slavery and pappy run 'way while he and Massa Bill on they way to the battle of Mansfield. Massa say when he come back from the war, 'That triflin' nigger run 'way and jines up with them damn Yankees.'

"Massa have six chillen when war come on and I nussed all of 'em. I stays in the house with 'em and slep' on a pallet on the floor, and soon I's big 'nough to tote the milk pail they puts me to milkin', too. Massa have more'n 100 cows and most the time me and Violet do all the milkin'. We better be in that cowpen by five o'clock. One mornin' massa cotched me lettin' one the calves do some milkin' and he let me off without whippin' that time, but that don't mean he allus good, 'cause them cows have more feelin' for than massa and missy.

4 Katie Darling, from *Slave Narratives: A Folk History of Slavery in the United States From Interviews*, vol. XVI, pp. 278-281. Copyright in the Public Domain.

"We et peas and greens and collards and middlin's. Niggers had better let that ham alone! We have meal coffee. They parch meal in the oven and bile it and drink the liquor. Sometime we gits some of the Lincoln coffee what was lef' from the nex' plantation.

"When the niggers done anything massa bullwhip them, but didn't skin them up very often. He'd whip the man for half doin' the plowin' or hoein' but if they done it right he'd find something else to whip them for. At night the men had to shuck corn and the women card and spin. Us got two pieces of clothes for winter and two for summer, but us have no shoes. We had to work Saturday all day and if that grass was in the field we didn't git no Sunday, either.

"They have dances and parties for the white folks' chillen, but missy say, 'Niggers was made to work for white folks,' and on Christmas Miss Irene bakes two cakes for the nigger families but she darsn't let missy know 'bout it.

"When a slave die, massa make the coffin hisself and send a couple niggers to bury the body and say, 'Don't be long,' and no singin' or prayin' 'lowed, jus' put them in the ground and cover 'em up and hurry on back to that field.

"Niggers didn't cou't then like they do now, massa pick out a po'tly man and a po'tly gal and jist put 'em together. What he want am the stock.

"I 'member that fight at Mansfield like it yes'day. Massas's field am all tore up with cannon holes and ever' time a cannon fire, missy go off in a rage. One time when a cannon fire, she say to me, 'You li'l] black wench, you niggers ain't gwine be free. You's made to work for white folks.' 'Bout that time she look up and see a Yankee sojer standin' in the door with a pistol. She say, 'Katie, I didn't say anythin', did I?' I say, 'I ain't tellin' no lie, you say niggers ain't gwine git free.'

"That day you couldn't git 'round the place for the Yankees and they stays for weeks at a time.

"When massa come home from the war he wants let us loose, but missy wouldn't do it. I stays on and works for them six years after the war and missy whip me after the war jist like she did 'fore. She has a hun'erd lashes laid up for me now, and this how it am. My brudders done lef' massa after the war and move nex' door to the Ware place, and one Saturday some niggers come and tell me my brudder Peter am comin' to git me 'way from old missy Sunday night. That night the cows and calves got together and missy say it my fault. She say, 'I'm gwine give you one hun'erd lashes in the mornin', now go pen them calves.'

"I don't know whether them calves was ever penned or not, 'cause Peter was waitin' for me at the lot and takes me to live with him on the Ware place. I's so happy to git away from that old devil missy, I don't know what to do, and I stays there sev'ral years and works out here and there for money. Then I marries and moves here and me and my man farms and nothin' 'citin' done happened."

2 Juan Cortina's Guerilla War in South Texas, 1859–1860

Juan Cortina is a complex figure in the history of Texas. He was born in 1824 in the Mexican state of Tamaulipas just south of the Rio Grande. His family owned a large amount of land of both sides of the Rio Grande near what today is the city of Brownsville, Texas. During the Mexican-American War (1846–1848) he fought with the Mexican Army against U.S. troops. The U.S. victory over Mexico and the signing of the Treaty of Guadalupe Hidalgo in 1848 established the Rio Grande as the border between the U.S. and Mexico and the annexed the territory of South Texas between the Nueces and Rio Grande as part of the United States. After living their entire lives under the Mexican flag, after 1848 those people living in this region suddenly became American citizens.

After 1848, Cortina settled in Texas to manage his mother's landholdings on the U.S. side of the river. During the 1850s, Cortina served as political boss in Brownsville and delivered votes to the Democratic Party. During that decade, however, he grew increasingly angry at the abusive treatment suffered by Mexican-Americans in South Texas. He was also outraged over the loss of a large portion of his family's land on the Texas side, which he blamed on a corrupt American political and judicial system that worked against Mexican-Americans.

In July 1859, Cortina shot a Brownsville sheriff whom he witnessed pistol-whipping one of his mother's elderly former employees. Cortina fled across the River to Matamoros, Mexico, but a few months later, in September, he returned to Brownsville with a group of 70 armed followers. Cortina returned to Brownsville with the intention on taking revenge on those he believed had killed Mexicans, including a man named Adolphus Glavecke. During his brief occupation of Brownsville, he killed four Anglos (Glavecke, however, survived), and freed a number of Mexican prisoners. In an odd turn of events, elements of the Mexican army crossed the Rio Grande to protect Brownsville from Cortina and his men. Cortina then withdrew to his mother's ranch.

This incident might have ended peacefully at that point, but a group of Texas Rangers sent to the border after the raid on Brownsville captured and lynched Tomás Cabrera, one of Cortina's chief lieutenants. The murder of Cabrera enraged Cortina and set off a six-month guerilla war in South Texas that pitted Cortina and his growing number of followers against the Texas Rangers and the U.S. Army. It was not until April of 1861 that Cortina, defeated by U.S. troops under the overall command of Colonel Robert E. Lee, withdrew into Mexico but not before leaving behind a trail of death and destruction that devastated South Texas. Within a few years after this event, Colonel Lee would gain international fame as the highest-ranking general in the Confederate Army. Historians still argue about Cortina. Some see him as a lawless bandit, but many, especially in South Texas, regard him as a borderlands Robin Hood fighting against pervasive Anglo racism.

The primary documents you are about to read come from Cortina and from the reports of U.S. Army officers sent to the border to suppress his insurgency. Cortina issued a number of *Pronunciamientos* (or proclamations) during the months of the so-called Cortina war to publically explain and justify his actions. These proclamations were widely disseminated by local newspapers. The first was written in September 1859 soon after his attack on Brownsville. The second was written in November 1859 after the death of Cabrera and the intensification of the guerilla war along the Rio Grande border.

The next group of primary sources you will read in this chapter were printed in an 1861 U.S. Congressional Report, "Troubles on the Texas Frontier." The first document was written as an overview of the situation written by the U.S. Army officer deployed to the border in 1860, Major

Samuel P. Heintzelman. (Note that Heintzelman spells Cortina's name as "Cortinas.") The second is a brief description of the loss suffered by a resident of the borderlands and includes his assessment of the effectiveness of the Texas Rangers sent to suppress Cortina. The third is Lee's letter politely declining the use of Texas Rangers in the effort against Cortina. The forth and fifth documents are the exchange between Robert E. Lee and Mexican officials in Reynosa, Mexico, a small community located on the Mexican side of the Rio Grande.

Section 1. Cortina *Pronunciamientos* Questions

1. Generally, how does Cortina justify his actions? Can you identify any specific grievances he has against U.S. and Texas authorities?
2. Who is Cortina's audience, Anglos or Mexican-Americans? Be prepared to discuss how you arrived at your decision concerning just who these proclamations were aimed at, who they were trying to convince.
3. How does Cortina describe the political, economic, and security situation of Mexican-Americans along the border in 1848?
4. What is the language that Cortina uses to describe the Mexican-Americans living along the border?
5. What is the language that Cortina uses to describe the Anglo Americans who he believes have unleashed a reign of terror on the Mexican-American citizens of South Texas.
6. Discuss Cortina's use of the word "race." How is he using this word, and what characteristics does he apply to the Anglo and Mexican-American "races"?
7. From your point of view as a student living in the twenty-first century, do you find Cortina's arguments persuasive?

Section 2. "Troubles on the Texas Frontier" Questions

1. In Major Heintzelman's report, do you find him sympathetic or unsympathetic to

the experience of Mexican-Americans along the border?

2. After reading his report, do you feel that Major Heintzelman offered Congress any insight as to why Mexican-Americans along the border might support Cortina?
3. Identify sections of this report where Major Heintzelman offers an understanding of the racial dimension of the Cortina war. Discuss his own use of racial language to describe the Mexican-American residents of the border.
4. According to Major Heintzelman, how did the lynching of Cabera escalate Cortina's actions in Texas?
5. As you read Heintzelman's report, F. M. Campell's letter, and Robert E. Lee's letter to George McKnight, consider whether or not U.S. Army officials and local residents felt that the Texas Rangers were an effective fighting force against Cortina.
6. Examine the role of Mexican troops in persuading Cortina to withdraw from Brownsville in September 1860.
7. Examine Lee's tone to Mexican officials in Reynosa. Do you find his letter more polite or threatening? What is Lee asking of Mexican officials?
8. Examine the response to Lee's letter by the *alcade* of Reynosa, Francisco Zepeda. How does Zepeda describe Cortina: as a hero or a nuisance?
9. In answering Lee, what does Zepeda indicate is the goal of Mexican authorities along the border.

Section 3.
Documents

Document 1

Juan Nepomuceno Cortina Pronunciamiento to the inhabitants of the State of Texas and especially to those of the city of Brownsville, Rancho Del Carmen, County of Cameron, September 30, 1859[1]

An event of grave importance, in which it has fallen to my lot to figure as the principal actor since the morning of the 28th instant; doubtless keeps you in suspense with regard to the progress of its consequences. There is no need of fear. Orderly people and honest citizens are inviolable to us in their persons and interests. Our object, as you have seen, has been to chastise the villainy of our enemies, which heretofore has gone unpunished. These have connived with each other, and form, so to speak, a perfidious inquisitorial lodge to persecute and rob us, without any cause, and for no other crime on our part than that of being of Mexican origin, considering us, doubtless, destitute of those gifts which they themselves do not possess... Our identity of origin, our relationship, and the community of our sufferings, has been, as it appears, the cause of our embracing, directly, the proposed object which led us to enter your beautiful city, clothes with the imposing aspect of our exasperation.

The assembly organized, and headed by your humble servant, (thanks to the confidence which he inspired as one of the most aggrieved,) we have careered over the streets of the city in search of our adversaries, inasmuch as justice, being administered by their own hands, the supremacy of the law has failed to accomplish its object.

Some of them, rashly remiss in complying with our demand, have perished for having sought to carry their animosity beyond the limits allowed by their precarious position. Three of them have died–all criminal, wicked men, notorious among the people for their misdeeds. The others, still more unworthy and wretched, dragged themselves through the mire to escape our anger, and now, perhaps, with their usual bravado, pretend

1 Juan Nepomuceno Cortinas, from *Difficulties on Southwestern Frontier*, pp. 70-72. Copyright in the Public Domain.

to be the cause of an infinity of evils, which might have been avoided but for their cowardice... These, as we have said, form, with a multitude of lawyers, a secret conclave, with all its ramifications, for the sole purpose of despoiling the Mexicans of the lands and usurp them afterwards. This is clearly proven by the conduct of one Adolph Glavecke, who, invested with the character of deputy sheriff, and in collusion with the said lawyers, has spread terror among the unwary, making them believe that he will hang the Mexicans and burn their ranches, &c., that by this means he might compel them to abandon the country, and thus accomplish their object. This is not a supposition–it is a reality; and notwithstanding the want of better proof, if this threat were not publicly known, all would feel persuaded that of this, and even more, are capable such criminal men as the one last mentioned, the marshal, the jailer, Morris, Neal, &c.

But, if necessary, we will lead a wandering life, awaiting our opportunity to purge society of men so base that they degrade it with their opprobrium. Our families have returned as strangers to their old country to beg for an asylum. Our lands, if they are to be sacrificed to the avaricious covetousness of our enemies, will be rather so on account of our own vicissitudes. As to land, Nature will always grant us sufficient to support our frames, and we accept the consequences that may arise. Further, our personal enemies shall not possess our lands until they have fattened it with their own gore.

It remains for me to say that, separated as we are, by accident alone, from the other citizens of the city, and not having renounced our rights as North American citizens, we disapprove and energetically protest against the act of having caused a force of the national guards from Mexico to cross unto this side to ingraft themselves in a question so foreign to their country that there is no excusing such weakness on the part of those who implored their aid.

Document 2

Cortina *Pronunciamiento*, November 23, 1859[2]

County of Cameron,
Camp in the Rancho del Carmen,

2 Juan Nepomuceno Cortinas, from *Difficulties on Southwestern Frontier*, pp. 80-82. Copyright in the Public Domain.

November 23, 1859

The Mexicans who inhabit this wide region, some because they were born therein, others because since the treaty Guadalupe Hidalgo, they have been attracted to its soil by the soft influence of wise laws and the advantages of a free government, paying little attention to the reasoning of politics, are honorably and exclusively dedicated to the exercise of industry, guided by that instinct which leads the good man to comprehend, as uncontradictory truth, that only in the reign of peace can he enjoy, without inquietude, the fruit of his labor. These, under an unjust imputation of selfishness and churlishness, which do not exist, are not devoid of those sincere and expressive evidences of such friendliness and tenderness as should gain for them that confidence with which they have inspired those who have met them in social intercourse. This genial affability seems as the foundation of that proverbial prudence which, as an oracle, is consulted in all their actions and undertakings. Their humility, simplicity, and doility, directed with dignity, it may be that with excess of goodness, can, if it be desired, lead them beyond the common class of men, but causes them to excel in an irresistible inclination towards ideas of equality, a proof of their simple manners, so well adapted to that which is styled the classic land of liberty. A man, a family, and a people, possessed of qualities so eminent, with their heart in their hand and purity on their lips, encounter every day renewed reasons to know that they are surrounded by malicious and crafty monsters, who rob them in the tranquil interior of home, or with open hatred and pursuit; it necessarily follows, however great may be their pain, if not abased by humiliation and ignominy, their groans suffocated and hushed by a pain which renders them insensible, they become resigned to suffering before an abyss of misfortunes.

Mexicans! When the State of Texas began to receive the new organization which its sovereignty required as an integrate part of the Union, flocks of vampires, in the guise of men came and scattered themselves in the settlements, without any capital except the corrupt heart and the most perverse intentions. Some, brimful of laws, pledged to us their protection against the attacks of the rest; others assembled in shadowy councils, attempted and excited the robbery and burning of the houses of our relatives on the other side of the river Bravo; while others, to the abusing of our unlimited confidence, when we entrusted them with our titles, which secured the future of our families, refused to return them under false and frivolous pretexts; all, in short, with a smile on their faces, giving the lie to that which their black entrails were meditating. Many of you have been robbed of your property, incarcerated, chased, murdered, and hunted like wild beasts, because your labor was fruitful, and because your industry excited the vile avarice which led them. A voice infernal said, from the bottom of their soul, "kill them; the greater will be our gain!" Ah! This does not finish the sketch of your situation. It would appear that justice had fled from this world, leaving you to the caprice of your oppressors, who become each day more furious towards you; that, through witnesses and false charges, although the grounds may be insufficient, you may be interred in the penitentiaries, if you are not previously deprived of life by some keeper who covers himself from responsibility by the pretense of your flight. There are to be found criminals covered with frightful crimes, but they appear to have impunity until opportunity furnish them a victim; to these monsters indulgence is shown, because they are not of our race, which is unworthy, as they say, to belong to the human species. But this race, which the Anglo-American, so ostentatious of its own qualities, tries so much to blacken depreciate, and load with insults, in a spirit of blindness, which goes to the full extent of such things so common on this frontier, does not fear, placed even in the midst of its very faults, those subtle inquisitions which are so frequently made as to its manners, habits, and sentiments; nor that its deeds should be put to the test of examination in the land of reason, of justice, and of honor. This race has never humbled itself before the conqueror, though the reverse has happened, and can be established; for his is not humbled who uses among his fellow-men those courtesies which humanity prescribes; charity being the root whence springs the rule of his actions. But this race, which you see filled with gentleness and inward sweetness, gives now the cry of alarm throughout the entire extend of the land which it occupies, against all the artifice interposed by those who have become chargeable with their division and discord. This race, adorned with the most lovely disposition towards all that is good and useful in the line of progress, omits no act of diligence which might correct its many imperfections, and lift its grand edifice among the ruins of the past, respecting the ancient traditions and the maxims bequeathed by their ancestors, without being dazzled by brilliant and false appearances, nor crawling to that exaggeration of institution which, like a sublime statue, is offered for their worship and adoration.... Mexicans! My part is taken; the voice of revelation whispers to me that to me is entrusted the work of breaking the chains of your slavery, and that the Lord will enable me, with powerful arm, to fight against our enemies, in compliance with the requirements of that Sovereign Majesty, who, from this day forward, will hold us under His protection. On my part, I am ready to offer myself as a sacrifice for your happiness; and counting upon the means necessary for the discharge of my ministry, you may count upon my cooperation, should no cowardly attempt put an end to my days.

Major Samuel P. Heintzelman to Colonel Robert E. Lee, March 1, 1861[3]

I reached Brownsville on the night of the 5th of December.

Juan Nepomosina Cortinas, (or Cortina) the leader of the banditti who have for the last months been in arms on the Lower Rio Grande, murdering, robbing, and burning, in a ranchero, at one time claiming to be an American, and at another a Mexican citizen. At the time General Taylor arrived on the banks of the Rio Grande, he was a solider in General Arista's army. He has been for years noted as a lawless, desperate man.

...He has a ranch called San Jose, a few miles from town, and whenever there was any danger of arrest he would retire to this place and keep himself surrounded by a band of outlaws, as desperate himself. Leading this lawless life, he and those around him made numerous enemies On the 13th of July last he was in Brownsville with some of his ranchero friends, when a man who was formerly a servant of his was arrested by the city marshal for abusing a coffee-house keeper. Cortinas attempted to rescue the man; he fired twice on the marshal, the second shot wounding him in the shoulder, and rescued the prisoner. He mounted his horse,

3 Samuel P. Heintzelman, from *Troubles on Texas Frontier*, pp. 2-7, 12-14. Copyright in the Public Domain.

took the prisoner up behind him, and with his friends around him rode off defying the authorities to arrest him. He escaped to Matamoras, and there was treated with consideration and lauded as the defender of Mexican rights.

Before daylight on the morning of the 28th of September Cortinas entered the city of Brownsville with a body of mounted men, variously estimated at from forty to eighty, leaving two small parties of foot outside—one near the cemetery, the others near the suburb of Framireno. The citizens were awakened by firing and cries of "Viva cheno Cortinas!" "Meusau los Gringos" "Viva Mexico!" The city was already in his possession, with sentinels at the corners of the principal streets and armed men riding about. He avowed his determination to kill the Americans, but assured Mexicans and foreigners that they should not be molested. Thus was a city of from two thousand to three thousand inhabitants occupied by a band of armed bandits, a thing till unheard of in these United States.

...He made his headquarters in the deserted garrison of Fort Brown, and sent mounted men through the streets hunting up their enemies. He broke open the jail, liberated the prisoners, knocked off their irons, and had them join him. He killed the jailer, Johnson, a constable named George Morris, young Neale in his bed, and two Mexicans; was after Glaseche, the wounded city marshal, and others. One of the his men was killed by the jailer, in the attack on the jail ... Cortinas himself rode up to a store on the levee and called for spirits of turpentine. A few minutes after this, General Caravajal made his appearance on the levee, and said that he would try and put a stop to all this, and seeing Don Miguel Tiguino on the opposite bank of the river, called to him to cross over to this side instantly. This he did, on horseback, accompanied by Don Agassito Longosia. General Caravajal then sent for Cortinas, and, after a talk with him, he with his men, mounted and on foot, numbering about sixty, marched along the levee out of towards his mother's rancho, about nine miles above the town.

His party did not make any attempt to plunder or rob, but were active in looking for the persons who had assembled to accompany the sheriff to arrest him, or for those who could be witnesses against him for former offences. Two of those killed had personal enemies amongst Cortinas' s men.

His sole object appeared to be revenge, but his men were getting liquor, and the consequences were only prevented by the exertions of the gentlemen above named and the Mexican consul, Don Manuel Tresino, in inducing him to leave the town. There were but thirty or forty native Americans in the place, and they mostly unarmed, and being taken completely by surprise, no effort was made to oppose him.There are said not to be over eighty American citizens, native or naturalized, in the two counties of Cameron and Hidalgo. Many of the foreigners in Brownsville refused to give any aid in its defense.

Two days after (30th of September) Cortinas issued his first proclamation, in which he bid defiance to law, and assumed to protect those whom he alleged had been injured on account of their Mexican origin, and accusing the lawyers of despoiling them of their lands.

After leaving Brownsville he encamped at his mother's rancho, and was there joined by stragglers from town, and Mexicans from the neighboring ranches. Several of the citizens of Matamoras and Brownsville now visited his camp, and had interviews with him. He appeared only to wish to have time to cross his property, stock & c., into Mexico. He took his time, without being molested, and then crossed with his men He and his men stayed about Matamoras publicly, unmolested by the authorities.

...About the 12th of October, several days after he left his side, the sheriff, with a posse, started up the river to visit his rancho, and to reconnoiter country. They caught Thomas Cabura, said to have been Cortina's second in command, on the 28th of September , and brought him in a prisoner. When Cortinas, who was in Matamoras, heard his, he told some of the most influential men there that if the citizens of Brownsville did not immediately release Cabura, that he would "lay the town in ashes, &c." A prominent merchant in Matamoras came over at 11 o'clock p.m., at the request of those Mexican gentlemen, to persuade the people of Brownsville to comply with his demand, whilst an express awaited, on the other side, their answer, to carry it to Cortinas. His demand was refused, but he was informed that the man was in the hands of the sheriff, to be dealt with by the laws of the country.

The night after the arrival of Captain Tobin's company Cabrera was found hung. Cortinas, with forty men, crossed the river the same night. He received their answer, and took up his old quarters, at his mother's rancho. Here he collected men and arms, and prepared to carry out his threats, occasionally sending threating communications to the authorities. His men would make their appearance on the outskirts of the town in open daylight; but the citizens had now organized and armed, and kept a guard day and night.

Some Mexican troops, who had been called over about the 30th of September, and who had returned home when Cortinas recrossed to the Mexican side, were now invited over again. About seventy-five men came over, with a piece of artillery, to join an expedition which the citizens were preparing for the purpose of attacking Cortinas. They were of the National Guards, of Matamoras, under the command of Colonal Loranco and Don Miguel Tigerino, who accompanied the expedition as a volunteer.

...The next day(25th) Captain Tobin again advanced, but when near the barricades there was another consultation, and it was decided to be imprudent to risk an attack, and the whole force marched back to Brownsville... It was a wise decision. In their disorganized condition an attack would have brought certain defeat. About a month before this the streets of Brownsville were barricaded.

...Cortinas was now a great man; he had defeated the "Gringos, " and his position was impregnable; he had the Mexican flag flying in his camp, and numbers were flocking to his standard. When he visited Matamoras he was received as the champion of his race—as the man who would right the wrongs the Mexicans had received; that he would drive back the hated Americans to the Nueces, and some even spoke of the Sabine and the future boundary. The lower order of Mexicans hate Americans, and the educated classes are not always exempt from this feeling. This is well shown from the difficulty we had in obtaining information. When his force and all his movements were well known in Matamoras, with daily intercourse with his camp, we were answered with vague and exaggerated accounts. Men who have lived here for years, and are united to Mexican women, could learn nothing reliable.

...Cortinas has been an outlaw and fugitive from justice for the last ten years. Some politicians found that he could influence a large vote amongst his countrymen, and during an election he was courted. Thus there was never any great effort made to bring him to justice. His mother owns ten leagues of land in a body near town, much of it covered with a dense chaparral. A few miles back from his house, near the river, he built a rancho called San Jose, which is arranged for a secure retreat, where it would be difficult to surprise any one. This was an asylum for horse and cattle thieves, robbers, and murderers, for those whose enemies would not permit them to live on the Mexican side of the river, or who dared not show themselves in the thickly settled parts of this State.

His first object in coming here was, no doubt, revenge to get ride of these. Then he would have gone off into the interior with some of his friends, in a government employment, until his deeds were forgotten. But the arrest of Cabrera, as he was ready to leave, kept him back. He recrossed the river to rescue Cabrera, and punish those who held him in custody. This idle and the dissolute flocked around him, lured by the prospect of plunder. He soon gained notoriety, and the affair grew beyond his control. The hatred of Americans on the frontier, amongst all classes of Mexicans, brought him men and means. Our side of the river furnished some horses and beef, with but few arms. Most of his arms, ammunition, and supplies to maintain his forces for so many months, came from Mexico, and principally from Matamoras. Most from his men were "pelados" from the towns from a market for his plunder. At Rio Grande City, in an ammunition box which we captured, were orders in which he is styled "General en Gefe," and he went about with a body guard.

The whole country from Brownsville to Rio Grande City, one hundred and twenty miles, and back to the Arroyo Colorado, has been laid waste. There is not an American, or any property belonging to an American, that could be destroyed in this large tract of country. Their horses and cattle were driven across into Mexico, and there sold, a cow, with a calf by her side, for a dollar.

At Rio Grande City, in answer to the complaints of his men that he had not fulfilled his promises, he told them that they should the next day have "manos libres" from ten to twelve. Our unexpected arrival saved the city from being sacked and burned, and the few Americans left from murder.

Rio Grande City is almost depopulated, and there is but one Mexican family in Edinburg. On the road this side I met but two ranchos occupied, and those by Mexicans. The jacales and fences are generally burned. The actual loss in property can give but a faint idea of the amount of the damage. The cattle that were not carried off are scattered in the chapparal, and will soon be wild and lost to their owners. Business, as far up as Lerido, two hundred and forty miles, has been interrupted or suspended for five months. It is now too late to think of preparing for a crop, and a whole season will be lost.

The amount of the claims for damages presented is three hundred and thirty-six thousand eight hundred and twenty-six dollars and twenty one cents; many of them are exaggerations, but then there are few Mexicans who have put in any.

There have been fifteen Americans and eighty friendly Mexicans killed. Cortinas has lost one hundred and fifity-one men killed; of the wounded I have no account.

...It will be a long time before the ill-feeling engendered by this out break can be allayed. It is dangerous for Americans to settle near their boundary. The river is narrow, and now low, and easy to cross. A robbery or murder is committed, and in a few minutes the criminal is secure from pursuit. Both banks must be under the same jurisdiction. It will at once add to the value of the lands and promote settlement. The industrious, enterprising, active race on one side cannot exist in such close proximity with the idle and vicious on the other without frequent collisions.

The class of the Mexican population (pelados) who joined Cortinas, are an idle, thriftless, thieving, vicious people, living principally on jerked beef and corn, a frijole as a luxury. The climate is such that they require but little in the way of clothing, or to shelter themselves from the weather, and the soil produces spontaneously much that they live upon. When they have enough to eat they only work on compulsion, which this system of peonage furnishes on the Mexican side of the river.

Document 4

F. M. Campbell to Captain J. B. Ricketts, Commander at Ringgold barracks[4]

Rio Grande City, January 28, 1860

4 F.M. Campbell, from *Troubles on Texas Frontier*, p. 19. Copyright in the Public Domain.

DEAR SIR: I see from a notice of Major L.S. Heintzelman, that all persons who have sustained damages from Cortinas or his command are requested to present them to him or to the commander at Ringgold barracks on or before the 21st day of January, 1860. I therefore respectfully represent that Cortinas took me prisoner about the 25th day of October last, and after keeping me in confinement ten days he released me, taking me from my horse, saddle, and bridle, one six shooter, one Sharpe's rifle, one bowie knife, and six dollars in cash. He also took from my ranch one gentle ox. The damages sustained by my improvement was much more than, the value of the property taken from me to say at least one thousand dollars.

I will also represent to you that I also received a heavy damage from the occupation of the Texas Rangers of my ranch near Brownsville. They burnt up my pens and fences for fire-wood, and one horse by accident. They also used a few hogs and goats and fifty barrels of sweet potatoes, and for which the commander refuses to pay me, although entreated to do so, and he cannot deny that they above articles were used, and that they took possession of my ranch and made use of my property without my consent.

I estimate the value of the property taken by Cortinas at fully two hundred dollars, and the value of property destroyed by Tobin's company at fully one thousand dollars, all of which are respectfully submitted by your obedient servant,

F.M.CAMPBELL

P.S.—It is notorious that Tobin bought no wood for this use of his men, although it could have been bought at a moderate rate.

F.M.C.

Document 5

Robert E. Lee to George McKnight, Headquarters Fort Brown, April 11, 1860[5]

Sir: I have had the honor to receive your letter of this date, transmitting a communication from his excellency the governor of Texas, and expressing

5 Robert E. Lee, from *Troubles on Texas Frontier*, p. 89. Copyright in the Public Domain.

his desire that the rangers now on the Rio Grande shall remain under my orders, provided the general government will assure their payment and subsistence. I have received no authority from the Secretary of War to receive into the service of the United States any portion of volunteers; and though sorry to part with troops that have performed good and efficient service in the disturbances on this frontier, I am yet unable to retain them on the conditions on you propose.

Under these circumstances, I am happy to inform you, for the information of his excellency the governor, that upon referring the subject of your letter to Major Heintzelman, who has conducted with much ability the military operations on the Rio Grande, he concurs with me in the belief that in the present condition of affairs the United States troops on the river will be sufficient to preserve order, provided the Mexican authorities are disposed to maintain peaceful relations with the United States, and will perform their duty. The services, then, of the rangers may at this time be more important on the Indian portion than on this.

I am, with great respect, your obedient servant,

R.E. Lee, Brevet Colonel,

Document 6

Robert E. Lee to the Civil and Military Authorities of the city of Reynosa, Mexico[6]

Gentlemen: In pursuance of instructions received from the honorable Secretary of War, of the government of the United States, I hereby notify you that you must break up and disperse the bands of banditti within your jurisdiction engaged in committing depredations upon the persons and property of American citizens, and that I shall hold you responsible for the faithful performance of this plain duty on your party

I have been informed that there are now within your jurisdiction armed followers of Cortinas, who were engaged in the recent outages committed by him on this side of the Rio Grande, prepared to make similar aggressions.

6 Robert E. Lee, from *Troubles on Texas Frontier*, p. 85. Copyright in the Public Domain.

This state of things cannot longer exist, and mist be put an end to.
I am, with high respect, your obedient servant.

R.E. Lee, Brevet Colonel, Commanding
Department of Texas.

Francisco Zepeda, Alcalde *of Reynosa, Mexico, to Robert E. Lee, April 8, 1861*[7]

In an extraordinary session held this day the corporation of this city has made itself acquainted with the contents of your esteemed letters of the 7th of April, addressed to the civilian and military authorities of the place, and has been decided to reply to you, through me, that if it be, indeed, quite certain that there are, unfortunately, within this jurisdiction any bandits of the Cortinas faction, which has been inflicted so much injury on the nation to which you belong—though to the sincere regret of all good Mexicans, who desire to have only the most pleasant relations with a friendly people—such criminals are yet mere skulking vagabounds, who sedulously keep out of the way of the authorities in pursuit of them; for you must known that the authorities of this city have orders from those above them to break up, pursue, arrest, and punish any and every band of men whom the factious Cortinas might attempt to collect on this side of the river, and on no account will any such be permitted to range undisturbed within this jurisdiction, but will, on the contrary, be consigned to a close prison, and turned over to their deserts; and to this end, an armed force has for such time past been scouring the district, with the exclusive object of hunting down all such malefactors.

The corporation has also requested me, sir, to call your attention to that certain persons, whether Mexicans or strangers is not known, have no scrupled to assure the authorities of the United States that the followers of Cortinas, or persons at least who are well affected to his cause, have been allowed to reside unmolested in this city, and that with such reports they have succeeded in creating injurious prejudices, and cause

7 Francisco Zepeda, from *Troubles on Texas Frontier*, pp. 85-86. Copyright in the Public Domain.

this neighborhood to live in the continued fear of an invasion of United States volunteer; whereas, in truth, the whole story is a fabrication, and the inhabitants of this city, and the country around it, have at heart no more sincere desire than to be allowed to live in peace, tranquility, and harmony with their neighbors across the river. In proof of which, I point to the fact that not one of the many Americans who have come here has ever sustained the slightest injury of any kind, but, on the contrary, whenever with their families they have come over here to invoke the protection of our town authorities, they have invariable received it.

3 A Woman's Personal Journey

Anita Dwyer Withers came from a prominent San Antonio, Texas family. She was married to military officer John Withers, who was serving as a captain in the U.S. Army prior to the start of the Civil War. He and Anita lived in San Antonio, but in September of 1860, the captain was called to Washington, D.C. Once the hostilities started, Withers resigned his commission in the U.S. Army and joined the Confederate forces where he rose in rank and served as an Assistant Adjutant General in Richmond, Virginia for Jefferson Davis, the president of the Confederacy. Between 1860 and 1865, Anita kept a journal that documented her daily life in Texas and Virginia. As a young wife and mother, she detailed the challenges, the petty annoyances, the simple pleasures, the joys, the fears, and the tragedies that marked her life and the lives of a nation torn apart by war.

Questions

1. Anita mentioned several prominent historical figures in her diary. She and her husband interacted with these figures. Who were some of the prominent people? What was Anita's opinion of them—can you determine this by what she wrote? Be familiar with the significance of the following people—particularly in regard to Texas history: Albert Sidney Johnston, David Emanuel Twiggs, and President John Tyler.

2. From the diary, can you determine Anita's social class? Her relationship with her family? Her relationship with her husband? Her education? Explain.
3. Her experience as a woman, mother, and officer's wife was quite complex. How would you describe her journey as a mother? How did she cope with loss? With physical pain? What challenges did she face as a woman? As an officer's wife, what expectations were placed on her?
4. What were the main components of her social life?
5. Her husband was a U.S. military officer. When the Civil War broke out, what factors might have influenced Anita and her husband in deciding to join the Confederate forces?
6. What were the pleasures in Anita's life? What were the annoyances?
7. Anita mentioned Civil War battles, victories, defeats, and deaths. Significantly, what people and events did she not mention or rarely mention?
8. Although John and Anita Withers lived in Texas, John Withers served in Virginia during the Civil War. In this way, Texas's being on the periphery of the war caused a very significant change in the Withers' lives. What were some of the consequences of this for Anita and her husband?

Document 1

Diary of Anita Dwyer Withers[1]

May 4, 1860–June 18, 1865
San Antonio, Texas and Richmond, Virginia
San Antonio, Texas.

May 4th. 1860.

1 Anita Dwyer Withers, from *Diary of Anita Dwyer Withers*, 1860-1865. Copyright in the Public Domain. Edited by Rhonda Minten.

May the 1st. was the first time that I went down to breakfast with my Husband since the birth of our baby. That morning I practised on the Piano, and took a ride in the afternoon.

May 4th.
All well (T G) Mrs. Mitchell, Miss Conrad, Miss Post, and Miss Rodriguez called to see me, they were all delighted with little Edward. We took a short drive. My Mother came over in the evening to take care of the baby so that I might go and hear the Swiss bell Ringers but I did not care to attend.

May 6th. [1860]
Sunday I went to Church this morning with the Captain for the first time since the birth of the baby, my Mother took care of him & nursed him on the bottle. Major Dashiell, Dr. D. his brother, and Miss Aurelia dined with us. Mrs. Williams had her children Baptised today by Mr. Bunting, we went round to her house, their were several persons there. We had cake and wine and spent an hour rather pleasantly; from there we went to see Mrs. Abbodie who arrived yesterday. Concion brought Mrs. Tabbin and Miss Navarro over to see me this afternoon. The Captain and myself were tired and came up stairs immediately after Tea.

May 9th. [1860]
A pleasant day. We went round to Menger Hotel to make a few calls in the afternoon. Mrs. Twigg and Sister Felicita came to see me for some collection they are making to build an Orphan's Asylum at New Braunfels, I gave her only five dollars, for I had no more to spare at present.

May 17th. 1860.
Thursday. A warm day, a feast of Obligation, The Ascension of our Lord. I went to Church this morning and came home in Capt. Lee's Ambulance that was standing near the Office. We took the baby to the Convent to see the children, the Nuns and all were greatly pleased with him, from there we went over to my Mother's, she was sick. Last evening we attended the party given by the ladies at the Menger, it was

an exceedingly pleasant one, nearly all the ladies & gentlemen of San Antonio were present & looked well. We came home at 1 o'clock and the baby did not cry once.

May 22nd. 1860.
Tuesday. Today the baby is two months old, his Papa weighed him and he has gained 2 lbs this last month. He now weighs 11 lbs. My Mother and Mr. Callaghan came to see him, Mr. Gallagher also called. The Capt. went up to the Hotel this afternoon, took a drive with Dr. Ford and brought him home to Tea. A number of persons called on me this evening.

June 1st. 1860.
Friday. I got up this morning feeling badly after the effects of the wedding. Concion was married last evening at the old church by Father Matteo. Mr. Tobin and Miss T. Navarro stood up for them. On our return from church we proceeded to the casita, there were quite a number of persons assembled, all relatives. I received a letter from Joe yesterday, he had just arrived in New York. The Captain and myself went over to see the bride this afternoon.

June 7th. 1860.
Thursday. I was sick nearly all the morning. Joe and my Ma came over after church, for it is the feast of Corpus Christi, they stayed until after dinner. They went to the Convent to see the little girls.

June 9th. 1860. Saturday.
I am again complaining today. My Ma and Joe staid here nearly all day. Miss Aurelia also came in from the country and remained all day.
Mr. Smyth took Joe to dine with him. In the evening they made some visits. My Mother and Joe staid to Tea, we had music after. The baby was vacinated.

June 11th. Monday. [1860]
Baby and I not very well. I was alone all day. The Capt. and I made some few calls in the afternoon. My Mother and Joe took Tea and spent the evening with us. We took a little walk around by the plaza after Tea.

June 12th. 1860. Tuesday.
Baby unwell—Doctor Herff came to see him. My Mother and Joe went out to the Ranch and spent the day. Joe returned quite sun-burnt.
June 14th. Thursday. [1860]
Baby and myself better. Ma and Joe spent the day here. In the afternoon I went out to invite for the Christening.

June 15th. [1860]
The Anniversary of our marriage, we have been married a year 1860. In the morning we arranged the house for an entertainment. Miss Aurelia and Mrs. Mickling came in today to assist me. They made the chicken salad & got Joe to help them. We set the table very prettily in the afternoon. I have had the headache all day, and got worse in the evening. I was obliged to leave the company and go upstairs to bed. About half past seven we went to the New Church with the baby, a great number of persons were already there. The Church was all lighted very prettily. Father Shean performed the ceremony. The party went off very well, although the Captain sent the Mexican musicians of. Joe played Robert on the Violin and I accompanied him on the Piano.

June 22ond. Friday. [1860]
The baby is three months old today. Mrs. N. sent shade for him. We took a drive this morning before breakfast, I don't feel very well this morning.

Mrs. Stein and children called. Mr. Williams also—Joe and my Mother came to Tea.

July 3rd. Tuesday. [1860]
Joe, my Mother and myself, baby and Charlotte went out to the Ranch—Joe acted driver, he went against a mesquite tree without seeing.

July 4th. Wednesday. [1860]
They had grand celebrations here procession and speeches. Joe and myself took a drive and went for the Captain. Mr. Williams came to see us in the afternoon. Mr. Gallagher came to tell us goodbye he is

going to the Virginia Springs. Miss Aurelia came down and spent the evening.

The Capt. & Joe went to the Ball given at the Casino.

July 11th. 1860. Wednesday.
I took a long drive with my Husband and baby—way round by the head of the river. My Ma and Joe spent the day with me. In the afternoon I made some calls.

July 16th. Monday. [1860]
We drove this morning towards the Missions—the looks well this morning. I made a few calls in the afternoon. Mr. Baylor and sister Tiny came to see us—he looked very sad.

July l9th. 1860. Thursday.
We took a drive towards the San Predro and met our friend as usual. In the afternoon I went to see Mrs. Devine, she collected a large bouquet of flowers for me. My Ma came over to Tea. Joe went to see Ada B.

July 20th. 1860. Friday.
We went out at six o'clock as usual. Joseph was quite busy all the afternoon trying to get up a party at the Menger Hotel. I made some calls.

Joe and the Captain went around to Mr. Nagels and Hansons after Tea. I went to bed. The baby did not wake once the whole night.

July 22ond. [1860]
Joe, my Ma and myself went to six o'clock Mass, I lost a little veil I had. Today the baby Edward is four months old, he weighs 13 and a half pounds. My Mother, the Capt, Joe, Myself, Charlotte with the baby went out to Major Dashiell's after our siesta. We had a nice moonlight drive returning. After Tea my Ma, Capt. and Joe commenced talking about the cattle on the Ranch, upon which topic my Mother got mad and went home.

August 1st. 1860. Wednesday.
We took our drive and went by the same old road again. Mrs. Duff invited us to her house this evening. The Capt. Joe, Miss A. and Mrs. Mickling

attended the party, it was delightful, we had a lovely night, moonlight, and an elegant supper.

August 3rd. Friday. [1860]
We neglected again to take our ride in the morning. Joe and myself went to visit, he hired an ambulance, my Ma and ourselves called on the Toutant family, and some others. We did not find the young lady as pretty as we expected. Since the party their has been a coolness between the Capt. and the S. ladies about something that he heard that they said. Last evening I think that they overheard the conversation that my husband and I had about them.

August 19th. Sunday. [1860]
The baby was sick and had high fever all night. Mr. Campbell, the gentleman that we invited to Tea yesterday, could not find the house and did not come. Major McClure came round to see us. I did not go to church today much to my regret, for the baby was sick and I was waiting for the Doctor until after 10 O'clock. Joe went out to the Rancho after dinner to bring my Ma in to see the baby.

August 22ond. [1860]
Baby somewhat better, the young men gave a party at the Menger, I was sorry not to be able to go, because the Captain seemed to be anxious to do so, but I had two very good reasons for not doing so.

August 23rd. Thursday. [1860]
The baby is a great deal better. My Mother has been over here all the week taking care of him. In the afternoon I took a ride on horseback with Col. Lee & Joe, we went round to hear the band first, and then went out in the country. Col. Lee remained to Tea.

August 27th. Monday. [1860]
We have a beautiful, clear, sunshiny day, good prospect for a party this evening. Ann and myself have been all the morning fixing a white silk dress of mine that I intend wearing to the party this evening. My Mother and Joe went home this morning. (Mr. Post died and was buried on Sunday.

August 28th. Tuesday. [1860]
I slept late this morning, for I felt very tired and sleepy after the party. I enjoyed the party exceedingly, there were only a few present, but with all that it went off very prettily. (Mrs. Sappington died.)

August 30th. Thursday. [1860]
In the morning before breakfast I took a ride on horseback with Joe. Afterwards about 10 O'clock I walked over to see Mrs. Kadaz and Mrs. Dashiells, the latter looks wretchedly. I don't think she is long for this world—

In the evening we had Dr. and Mrs. Abadie, Captain Blair, Clitzs, Mr. Edgar & Miss Ash. We spent a very pleasant evening considering that I was so sick and tired running about, for Ann got drunk and was quite stupid, I had to send for [?] The baby had fever yesterday but is better now. I invited Ada Bradly and Col. Lee last evening, but they did not come.

August 31st. Friday. [1860]
I remained at home all the morning. The baby is not well. Mrs. Washington and Mrs. Dr. Howard called on me & asked to see the baby.

In the evening I was angry and put out about Anne breaking another of my fine goblets. We went round to Mrs. Abats after tea, and met Mr. Baylor, Mr. Wade and Mr. Edmunds. We all played and had quite a musical entertainment. Miss Emilie accompanied Joe on the Piano, she plays extremely well.

September 1st. 1860.
Saturday. Melinda, our cook, left us this morning, I had to send for Margaret to make dinner for us until we got a servant. Capt. told Ann that she had to leave soon also. Mr. Echols came to see me, also Mrs. Lewis and nieces. After Tea I took a moonlight ride on horseback. Joe was my escort as usual. My Ma came over late in the evening & bought Edward a pretty little hat.

Sept. 6th. 1860.
The Captain received an order to go to Washington quite unexpectedly to us. I regret it mightily.

Sept. 13th. [1860]
Thursday we spent at home, the last day with my Mother.

Sept. 14th. 1860. Friday.
We left home for Washington by the way of Columbus. My brother came a part of the way with us. I hated to leave my Mother and home greatly.

October 3rd. 1860.
Wednesday. We arrived in Washington, & stopped at Brown's where we spent nearly a fortnight. My baby sick all the time, Dr. Edwards is attending him.

Oct. 19th. [1860]
The baby is much better this morning—he had a good night's rest. Mr. Calvert spent the evening and took Tea with us.

November 6th. [1860]
Mr. Lincoln I regret to say is elected President of the United States. What will become of us.

Thursday 15th. [1860]
We went to hear Jefferson in the American Cousin, I was greatly pleased, but what amused me most was the English Lord of Londreary acting the silly "Thats the idea." We drove home in a carriage.

Tuesday 20th. [1860]
We went to hear G. Christy the Negro Minstrels, they had a crowed house. I found very amusing, they had some very good Music.

The Captain went to Charleston Dec. 21st. & returned on Christmas Day.

March 1st. 1861.
The Captain resigned on the 7th. March 1861. We left Washington on the 13th. for Huntsville, where we spent two weeks. About April the 8th. the C— accepted the same position in the Confederate Army which he had in the old one.

We moved to Mrs. Ponder 29th. April—and left for Richmond where the seat of Government was changed to on the 30th. May.

June 1st. 1861.
We arrived in Richmond on the 2ond of the month & stopped at the Spotswood, the same place where President Davis and family stayed. We moved to Mrs. Duval's on 5th. We are very much pleased with the house and boarders.
Edward walked for the first time on the 8th. of June, The Capt. and myself were exceedingly delighted to see him, he was just fourteen months and half old when he made his first attempt.

June 15th. [1861]
The anniversary of our marriage. We were married two years today, and Eddie was christened a year ago.

June 22ond. Saturday. [1861]
Edward was 15 months old today, he is better now than I have seen him for months, he has another tooth nearly through.

July 1861.
The fourth was celebrated here in a very quiet way. Eddie was taken sick suddenly last night about twelve O'clock, he suffered very much, we were up with him all night. The next morning we called Dr. Brewer to see him, who stays in the house, he got better by the afternoon. Mrs. Duval was exceedingly kind, she nursed him nearly all day.

Wednesday 10th. [July, 1861]
Eddie was very ill all day, I packed my trunk to go to the Springs with him. In the Afternoon Mrs. Toombs and Mrs. Brown called to see me. Mrs. T. was exceedingly kind, offered to come and sit up with Eddie at night. Miss Lee and Mrs. Warrick also called.

I sent Eddie round to the Square, he couldn't even hold his little head up.

Thursday 11th. [July, 1861]
We had a terrible night last night. My baby was extremely ill, nauseated so much that we thought he could not possibly stand it. Mrs. Govan came up about 2 O'clock hearing him cry so pitifully. Dr. Brewer was waked up to see him, and ordered a black blister to be put on him for two hours and half, that seemed to relieve him more than anything else.

About 10 O'clock Dr. Conway was called in to see him, he told me Eddie was a very sick child but still there was nothing alarming in his symtoms.

Sunday 14th. [July, 1861]
Eddic did not spend a good night, seemed to be in pain all the time, this morning I did not go to Church, stayed at home with Eddie all day.

Mrs. Johnston & McLane called on me yesterday.

On Thursday 18th. July The Captain had to call in Dr. Conway again, for we thought little Eddie sicker and very feeble. On Friday the darling got very low, by evening we could not warm his little feet and hands. I was all ready and packed yesterday (deed have been for the last week) to go out to the country, mountains, or in any direction that could benefit my Angel, but the Physicians objected to my going. I suppose they knew all the time that my babe was too ill.

Friday afternoon such a change took place that I had very little or no hope of the baby's recovery.

Mrs. Dr. Wait was kind enough to send me round her carriage. Dr. Conway was in at the time, so he told us to take Edie out to drive, it could hurt him. I went with a aching, agonizing heart, expecting every moment for my child to go off. I never shall forget that ride and that evening as long as I live. I weeped all the time.

That night Dr. C. ordered us to give him 20 drops of Paregoric as a last resort or remedy, to produce sleep. Mrs. Duval, who was a kind, good friend to us all during his sickness, assisted us in nursing that his last night in this world of sorrows and troubles. My own precious suffered terribly all night, he could not get any rest for more than 10 minuits at a time. I could scarcely control myself, my anxiety and pain of mind and heart were terrible.

Saturday 20th. [July, 1861]
My own babe was gradually and quietly fading away, like a little Angel that he was, travelling to his Heavenly Home, where no pain, sickness, or sorrow will ever reach him.

Bishop McGill came just a few moments before my babe departed, which was about three O'clock in the afternoon. The Bishop tried to comfort and console us, but it was difficult at that time of intense grief and anguish of heart. I felt as if they were tearing my soul from my body. He was layed out in the little room. Col. Chilton and watched that night. The next day he was put in the coffin, buried on Sunday afternoon, the day the Grand battle at Manassas was fought. The Bishop read the Funeral Service in the parlour, and made a beautiful address, I did not go down but the ladies told me. The parlour was crowded with ladies and gentlemen, Mrs. President Davis, Mrs. Johnston, Mrs. Wigfall, and McLean had the politeness to attend. My own was layed in the Bishop's Vault, so as to take him home with us when we return. That same Sunday night The Captain took me round to Mrs. Nelson's, I went stait up to bed. We spent a whole week there, with exception of one day and night that we spent at Mr. Williams'. Mrs. Nelson and all the ladies were exceedingly kind to us.

Sunday the 28th. [1861]
We went to late Mass, I was in deep black. The Bishop gave a beautiful Sermon.

The Southern Congress met here the day that my own darling died.

August 11th. Sunday. [1861]
The Captain and myself went to St. Peter's Church. We had a fine sermon by Bishop McGill "On Charity."

After Church we walked round to Mr. John Purcell's for a little while returned home and read a letter from Angel. How strange things happen in this world. Concion's little girl was born on the day that my Angel Boy was buried. I felt miserable the rest of the day, in fact all the time I have felt loneliness and sadness. (Col. Burwell called to see us—

On the 15th, Feast of the Assumption, I attended Mass at 8 O'clock.

Sunday 18th. August. [1861]
The Captain and myself went to Church at ten O'clock. A new and Young Priest preached a pretty good Sermon but timidly and hurriedly.

On Thursday the 22nd The Captain and myself went round to the Bishop's this morning a little while to try and get the key of the Vault, he directed us to go to the Sexton.

In the Afternoon The Captain, Charlotte & myself went out to the cemetery, it is a desolate looking place where my babe is buried, but I hope we will soon take him home.

Sept. 3rd. Tuesday. [1861]
I went to Mrs. Nelson's in the morning, took my nitting & remained for about three hours. I met Mrs. Dr. Wayt there, she invited to Tea the next evening. Captain and Mrs. Williams called in the evening to see us, there was quite an excitement, a poor old Negro man was robbed and beaten on the street, he made a great noise. The Gentlemen ran to his assistance.

Friday 6th. (1861)
General Sidney Johnson arrived here, with Major Howard as did I went around to the Office in the evening with the Captain—

Saturday 7th. [1861]
All day at home. In the evening Captain Myers took his wife, Mrs. Brewer & myself to Pizzinis to get some ice cream. My Husband did not come until after eleven he was kept on bus—— with Gen. Johnson.

Sunday Sept. 22ond. [1861]
My babe would have been one year & half old today. The Captain and myself went to Church at ten O'clock. Bishop McGill preached a beautiful Sermon on the "Forgiveness of sins" or Confession. In the Afternoon I went to Vespers and to see Mrs. Stewart. My Husband walked back home with me.

Monday 21st. [Oct. 1861]
We had a grand victory over the Yankees at Leesburg. Captain Evans commanded and behaved splendidly. I commenced to knit a Sontag for Cousin Celeste. I went out to see Mrs. Washington. In the afternoon Mrs. Dr. Wayt took me to drive. We saw the North Carolina Regiment of Calvary reviewed by the President.

Monday 4th. [1861]
We were invited to Mr. John Purcell's to Tea, they had quite a large entertainment, and fine supper.
Wednesday—Mr. Limbough & John Elliot called to say Goodbye—Johnny is going to Mannassas. In the afternoon I went round to Mrs. Nelson's. I had two letters on the 5th. from home.
Mr. Washington is going away in the morning and leave his wife.

Thursday 21st. [Nov. 1861]
I went to the Dentist, Dr. Wayt, this morning, and had 4 teeth plugged. Mrs. Wayt sent me an elegant lunch, which I did not eat until two O'clock.

Mrs. Williams, Washington, and baby called on me. In the afternoon Mrs. Nelson and Maury came round. The Captain & myself went round to Mrs. Nelson's to Tea. Dr. and Mrs. Curtis are staying there. Mrs. Gen. Stuart and children came this evening to stay her for the winter. I bought a new bonnet today.

Thursday 28th. [Nov. 1861]
I went round to Dr. Wayt's this morning, he finished fixing my teeth & pulled out one. The Captain went to a concert that Mr. DeCorneil gave for the benefit of the Soldiers, I did not go for the evening was very damp and raining.

Monday 9th. [Dec. 1861]
The Captain and myself made a few calls in the afternoon.

On Tuesday we were invited to the wedding, it did not come off, both lady & gentleman being under age they had to run off to North Carolina to get married.

Christmas Day 25th. [Dec.] Wednesday. [1861]
We went to Church at 10 O'clock. Father McMullen preached a very good sermon. After Church we all went to Mr. John Purcell's and took a glass of egg-nog, and from there we went to see the Sisters, Mrs. Randolp took us ladies in her carriage. (The Stable of Bethlehem was beautiful.) The little Orphans sang for us. About five we walked up to Mr. Menard's to dine—we returned about nine.

Wednesday. January 1st. [1862]
New Year's day was a lovely day—quite mild but windy. We went to Church at 10 O'clock. Father Andrews preached. After Church Captain and myself walked up to see Mrs. Williams, she had been sick and was looking wretchedly—she made a nice egg-nog for us. From there The Capt. and Mrs. Williams walked with me to Mrs. Nelson's where I remained until they returned from the President's, who had a Reception. Crowds of people passed by. The band played some pretty airs.

Sunday 5th. [Jan. 1862]
My birthday, I completed my 23rd. year today. The Capt. gave me a beautiful cake. We went to Church at eleven.
I dressed finely for dinner, after which we invited Dr. and Mrs. Brewer to take a glass of wine and cake with us. Major Williams came round to see us. Poor Judge Hemphill is dead.

January 6th. [1862]
Feast of the Epiphany. The ground is covered with snow. I went to Church at ten. Father Androws preached a good sermon.

Saturday 18th. [Jan. 1862]
I took my lesson. I have just heard of the death of poor Ex-President Tyler.

Sunday 9th. February. [1862]
I was taken sick, had high fever all night, and continued to have it for a week. I had a terrible attack of pneumonia and a miscarriage. I layed dangerously ill for several days. Dr. Dean felt very uneasy about me. My dear Husband nursed me tenderly through my sickness. One evening

we talked about Religion, he promised me seriously he would try and become a member of the Catholic Church. Mrs. Duval and Mrs. Stuart were extremely kind to me. They used to dress my blisters & poultices. Mrs. Wootten, another kind friend, arranged my hair for me every morning for a week. All my other friends outside were exceedingly kind to me also in coming to see me, and sending me nice things to tempt my appetite.

Cousin Jeannie & Clement arrived here on the evening of the 18th. of Feb. The day the permanent Congress met. I was still confined to my bed when they came. Cousin Lawson was also in the city for a few days, on his to Knoxville, Tenn.

March 1st. Saturday. [1862]
I walked into the parlour this morning for the first time in several weeks.

Saturday 22 March. [1862]
My Angel boy would have been 2 years old today. I took a Music lesson—remained at home all day.

May 1st. 1862.
Thursday, the Captain left for Richmond this evening. I don't believe I can go to Texas if New Orleans is surrendered.

The Capt. telegraphed to me on Sunday, June 1st. to go to Rich— by first opportunity.

My friends advise me not to leave until we hear of the result of the battle. I feel very anxious about my Husband.

Capt. Myers is also in Richmond.

May 31st. [1862
Salisbury.
The battle near Richmond commenced today—as far as we have heard they have continued fighting for three days.

June 2nd. [1862]
I have written to the Capt. and sent the letter by persons going.

Mrs. Myers and myself went to the depot this evening to hear the news. They have stopped fighting to bury their dead.

June 7th. Saturday. [1862]
I left Salisbury, Mr. Burke was my escort.

June 8th. [1862]
I reached Richmond this evening after a fatiguing ride. My Husband was down to the depot to meet me. I went straight to bed with a sick headache. In my old room on the third story again.

June 26th. Thursday. 1862.
This grand battle near Richmond commenced this morning under command of General R. Lee. Gen. Jackson sent in the rear of the enemy.

We took Mechanicsville the first day, one of the enemies best positions.

June 27th. [1862]
The enemy retreated several miles,—it is reported we are whipping them.

June 28th. Saturday. [1862]
The battle is progressing favourably to us, I understand. We have captured several thousand prisoners, numbers of officers high in rank.

June 29th. Sunday. [1862]
The Yankees reported running towards the James River, our forces after them. Everything seems pretty quiet in the city today. I went to Church at ten O'clock this morning. Father Andrews preached.

Tuesday July 1st. 1862.
Mr. Pulaski came in from camp and informed us that poor Mr. Abbot was killed the previous night, soon after this his body was brought to the house in an old wagon covered with straw, he was shot through the head, and of course very much disfigured. No person saw him but the gentlemen. My Husband assisted in dressing and cleaning him. Poor fellow, a nobler heart never lived, he supported his Mother, Wife and child. Little Walter is only thirteen months old. Mrs. Duval has been away during all

this sad and distressing time, she went to see her Sisters who have lost their two brothers.

Wednesday 2ond. July. [1862]
Poor Mr. Abbot was buried this morning at 10 O'clock. It was pouring down raining all day long.

Mrs. Shober from Salisbury came in to see me, she came to see after her brother's remains, Major Wheat.

July 4th. [1862]
No more news from the enemy except that they are still retreating and we pursuing them.

The fourth was not celebrated I don't expect by either side.

Tuesday 15th. of July. [1862]
Today is a very hot day. I walked out to Church at eight o'clock. About 1 O'clock The Capt. came home and brought Gen Hood with him, they took a drink and a little lunch. Capt. Myers came in also.

We had a delightful shower in the evening—We remained at home.

We heard that poor old General Twiggs died today in Augusta, Georgia.

Monday 21st. [July, 1862]
Mr. Niendoff and Mr. Snowdon came to see me today. Mr. N. returns to Texas tomorrow, I write to my Mother by him—

Thursday 28th. [August, 1862]
My Husband arrived today quite unexpectedly. I was mighty glad to see him. A delightful day it is.

Friday 29th. [August, 1862]
A pleasant day. We have nice dancing now since the Capt. came to see me. Mrs. Cranz, Kent Fishbourne and myself.

Saturday 30th. [August, 1862]
My husband had a letter from Major Whiting today, he will have to return to Richmond tomorrow, Sunday.

August. 1862. Sunday 31st.
My Husband is getting ready to leave torectly.

We had a letter from my brother the other day, he says he is going to get married very soon to Miss Annette Magoffin.

My Husband left me on Sunday, 31st. of August.

A Grand battle fought at Manassas on that day, Gen. Lee in command.

Sept. 8th. [1862]
I received two letters from my Husband today, and one he sent me from my Uncle Tom. the day is very, warm—I expect to start for Richmond tomorrow about twelve O'clock.

Sept. 9th. Tuesday. [1862]
We left Coyners today, we have had quite a pleasant time there—

We arrived in Rich— on Wednesday—about 5 O'clock—my Husband met me at the depot all seemed glad to see me—

Monday 15th. [1862]
My Husband went to the battle field with Mr. Purcell and Menard and spent the day riding about.

I called on Mrs. Morris & Mrs. Purcell.

Tuesday 16th. [1862]
A warm day—We've had a fight at Harper's ferry—

Oct. 5th. Sunday. [1862]
We had a letter from Joe yesterday in which he mentioned he expected to be married on the 4th. day of September.

Tuesday. 18th. [Nov. 1862]
It rained, and so it continued all the rest of the week.

Joe went up to Gen. Lee's Army—I feel badly nearly all the time.

Saturday 22ond. [Nov. 1862]
This morning we went down to see the Gunboat Richmond. Joe's brothers-in-law have arrived here. Gen. Sibley is soon expected—

1st. Dec. [1862]
Tuesday evening the Capt. and Joe went to Mr. Davis's, the President, had a cup of Tea.

Thursday 4th. December. [1862]
Joe had his likeness taken. He left us and started for Texas. I wish we could have gone with him.

Friday, Dec. 19. [1862]
We have again whipped the Yankees at Fredericksburg. They are fighting also at Kingston, in N. Carolina.

Wednesday 24th. [Dec. 1862]
Christmas eve. Major Whiting is dangerously ill. Dr. Dunn & Dr. Peachy are attending him—

Christmas morning at four O'clock Major Whiting died, his wife came down and asked my Husband to go up—when he got there the poor man had expired—he was delerious during his whole sickness—

Christmas day I went to Church at half past ten. My Husband was busy and could not go—he had to attend to every thing for Mrs. Whiting, her husband had to be buried the same afternoon—

It was the saddest Christmas I ever spent—no person dined out, though many were invited. We were to have dined at Mr. John Purcell's.

Friday 26th. [Dec. 1862]
I went up to see Mrs. Whiting, it excited me a good deal—I felt very badly all day.

By night I felt quite sick, dreadful pains in my limbs. My Husband went round to Major Williams to drink Egg-Nogg, Mrs. Govan and Mrs. Abbott sat with me until ten O'clock.

Saturday 27th. [Dec. 1862]
I was sick in bed all day, Dr. Dean came to see me. Mrs. Whiting went over to Mrs. Ives this morning.

Monday 29th. [Dec. 1862]
I am much better today. It is amost lovely day. In the afternoon my Husband and myself went for Mrs. W. and took her to see her Husband grave.

New Year's day, Jan'y 1st. Thursday. [1863
Was a most lovely day. I felt perfectly miserable, as sick as I could be. My Husband took me out riding in the afternoon, Mrs. Govan went with us. Dr. Dean came to see me in the evening—he would not give me any medicine but told me to go out all the time—

January 5th. [1863]
My birthday, I am 24 years old today.

I went to Holy communion early this morning. I came home quite sick— My Husband gave me a nice large cake and apples. I am going to Dr. Wayt's farm tomorrow.

Tuesday 10th. February [1863]
Mrs. Semmes gave a delightful party. We enjoyed it very much, we met all the elit of Richmond there.

Sunday 22 of Feb. [1863]
My Husband's birthday. I had nothing to give him. It has been snowing heavily all day long. I could not get to Church.

I had my mouseline dress dyed for $2. and made it up myself. 23—24 —25th.

Sunday. April 5th. Easter [1863]
It is a very disagreable day, snowing & raining. I went out to Church at 8—went to Holy communion and returned at nine and half.

Friday 1st. May. [1863]
A most lovely day. The enemy crossed, and were fighting near Fredericksburg yesterday. I came into town with Mrs. Pelaski. We had some delicious Ice cream & cake for dinner, it was the Anniversary of Mrs. Duval's wedding.

Saturday 2nd. [May.][1863]
I went to Church early. I went out calling with Cousin Jeannie, came home quite tired.

Gen. Lee's Army has defeated the Yankees again near Fredericksburg—May 4th. & 5th.

I again went to Church at 5 O'clock. After Tea the Capt. went round to the President's—

Sunday 3rd. May. [1863]
We went to Church, after which I went home with Mrs. James Purcell. We came home at 4 O'clock, took a nap. In the evening we heard a hundred rumours about the Yankees coming to Richmond, only 15 miles from here, it is reported,—the people all seem to be very much excited. Cousin Jeannie speaks of going home day after tomorrow.

Sunday 10th. [May 1863]
General Jackson died of his wounds and pneumonia. The great and noble hero will be a great loss to our country. Stonewall Jackson's remains will be brought down today, Monday.

Tuesday 12th. [May 1863]
Gen. Jackson's remains were removed, they had an immense military procession through the streets, the stores and offices were all closed.

Sunday 17th. [May 1863]
We went to Church at 8 O'clock. I have been to see Mrs. John Purcell who has a young baby.

It is reported that Jackson, Missis. has fallen.

Monday 15th. June. [1863]
We have been married four years today. I walked up to Dr. Brewer's about 12 O'clock. Capt. Myers and my Husband dined with us, we had a delicious dinner we an enjoyed it. In the evening Capt. Myers took Cousin Jeannie and myself to Pezzinis—

I have had delightful news from home today, John Elliot has written to my Husband saying that Maria, my sister, was expected in San Antonio daily from Europe. It seems Father Dubuis has been made Bishop and brought her out.

Friday 26th. [June, 1863]
A gloomy day. General Lee's Army is in Maryland.

In the afternoon I made one or two visits—spent the evening at Mrs. Grant's—The Yankees have made another cavalry raid.

Sunday 28th. June. [1863]
I went to Church at 8 O'clock— received Holy communion. After Church and breakfast the Captain went out to Camp to quiet some Mississippi troops that became insurbordinate—

July 1st. Wednesday. [1863]
We received a letter from Angel—they were all torably well at home when he wrote.

I got up this morning feeling a little badly—walked out and remained all day at Mrs. James Purcell's, spent a pleasant day and had a good dinner.

I came home and found a number of presents from friends—

Thursday 2 July. [1863]
There has been a deal of excitement in the city about Yankees coming. The Militia has been ordered out.

Mrs. John Purcell called on me.

In the evening we walked out to Antonis and had some delicious ice cream.

The weather is intensely hot—

July 3rd. [1863]
A very hot day. The Militia is out again today. I felt very badly all the evening, retired about ten O'clock.

July 4th. 1863.

Last night I did not rest well, I felt uncomfortable all night long,—waked up very early, sent for Dr. Dean before breakfast, he said there was no doubt but that I was in labour. Aunt Sally, the nurse, Mrs. Duval and my Husband were with me—the baby was born about a 15 minutes after eleven—not a Doctor was near me, Dr. Dean being engaged with Mr. Wall's wife who had a daughter on the same day.

Dr. Cunningham can to see me the first day—Dr. Talley was also sent for but was too late.

Our dear little Johnny is a fine little fellow, weighed nearly eight lbs. My friends were exceedingly kind to me, sending me nice things, and coming to see me. I had company nearly every day until I left Mrs. Duval's.

The Semmes left whilst we were there. The house was exceedingly noisy and disagreeable during my confinement, if it had not been for Mrs. Duval kindness we could have stood it.

Mrs. Tom Williams had a boy born on the same day as mine—likewise called after his Father.—

I heard my brother had a daughter born a month previous to mine.

We moved up to Mr. Starke's on the 1st. August, Saturday, we had an exceedingly hot spell when we first went up, however the change was pleasant, we live a good deal better. Mrs. Starke is very kind—the water we have up here is delightful.

August 15th. Saturday. [1863]
I had my baby christened today by the Bishop, who stood as god-father, and Miss Emily Mason God-Mother. We returned home and had some champagne and cake—

Vicksburg fell on the day the baby was born—

September 1st. [1863]
We find it very pleasant at Mr. Starke's—

Tuesday we spent the day at Mrs. Tom Williams' very pleasantly. My boy is much larger than hers, fatter although born on the same day. Capt. Myers sent us a box of peaches.

The second Wed—We went to see Mrs. Duval and Mrs. Hall—Charlotte went back and Pattie came.

Sep'r 8th. Tuesday. [1863]
We spent a very pleasant day at Mrs. John Purcell's—had a nice dinner and enjoyed everything—

October 1st. Thursday. [1863]
We hired a girl that belonged to Col. Garnett to nurse Johnnie, Louisa is just from the country and seems to be a good servant—We have had a great deal of trouble with servants, I have been worried to death—

October 3rd. Saturday. [1863]
We moved to Mrs. Nelson's—we are elegantly fixed—better off than we ever have been in Richmond, in every respect. We occupy the whole of the third floor.

We have just received a box from sister with some wine and other little things—

Saturday 17th. [October, 1863]
We are very pleasantly fixed at Mrs. Nelson's. I went around to Mrs. Duval's and saw them all there. I took little Johnny there, nicely dressed, they all made a great fuss over him.

There is a report that they are fighting up in the army.

Sunday, October 18th. [1863]
I have just returned from Church. The Capt. I believe has gone to the country with Mr. Grant. A great many rumours on the street, the Militia is going up to Western Virginia.

I have not heard from my home for months.

October 23rd. Friday. [1863]
Rather pleasant. I received three letters from home, one from Maria— all well. Joe has a boy named Edward, Concion one called Eugene. Grand doings at home—I wish I was at home. I feel very homesick.

Mrs. Dangerfield finished my light poplin today—it wants altering very much. Dear little Johnny was sick yesterday, but better today—he has taken cold.

Sunday, November 1st. 1863.
Feast of All Saints. A beautiful day. The Capt. is going out to the country to Mr. Grant's to spend the day. We bought a servant yesterday, I trust she may suit us. Susan seems to be a good natured women, and says she is only eighteen—

I had several letters from home a few days ago, they were all well there.

Johnny is a fine healthy little boy—the poor little fellow will have to part with his nurse Louisa—

Nov. 28th. [1863]
Susan seems to get along pretty well. Johnny knows her already. I have had one of my dreadful sick headaches lately, I feel very weak from it.

Mrs. & Captain Myers came from Salisbury to stay with us on 19th. December. We had a very pleasant time together, going every day.

On Christmas day Col. Williams & his family, Capt. Wade & Capt. Myers & wife dined with us. We had a mighty nice dinner—cake, Jelly, Blanc Mange and many nice things.

The gentlemen gave several parties. My Husband was invited to Mr. Grant's, Maury's and Dr. Cabell's.

Capt. and Mrs. Myers left us on the 4th. January, they hated to leave us and Richmond.

January 4th. [1864]
Johnny was six months old today.

January 5th. [1864]
I am twenty five years old today. I had some cake and wine handed round.

Mr. Bunting from San Antonio called to see me. In the evening Myer Myers came to see us—

January 20th. [1864]
We have had a most delightful spell of weather for two weeks past,

mild & balmy & springlike, very unusual for this place at this season of the year—

Poor Mrs. Govan lost her only son, & Mrs. Branch her brother Mr. Bulkley. I attend the former funeral.

Feb. 4th. [1864]
Johnny was seven months old today, he cannot sit alone yet—nor has he got a single tooth—the poor little follow has taken a most wretched cold and cough & has been very restless at night.

The Capt. attended a play at Colonel Ives the other evening—Cousin Virginia and Celeste took part and acted their parts admirably well I am told. I could not go, not being very well, nor the baby well enough for me to leave him—

February 25th. Thursday. [1864]
A rather mild but a windy and disagreeable day—Dr. Dean came to see me this morning, he advises me to wean Johnnie and get a wet nurse if possible. I dislike it greatly, but I expect will have to do it.

Johnny has cut his first two front tooth without any sickness, I am happy to say. We found them for the first time on Sunday last, the twenty first.

I would give a great deal to see my dear Mother, and relations once more, but I fear I will not be able until after the war.

Thursday, 3rd. March [1864]
The Yankees made a grand raid near Richmond, expected to have captured and hung Jeff Davis and Cabinet, and set fire to Richmond. Their expedition failed altogether, thank God, and about three hundred of them were captured.

Friday 4th. [March, 1864]
My Johnny is eight months old today, he has been quite unwell for the last two days cutting teeth. I went to see Mrs. Finch, Mrs. Harrison, & Miss Webb.

I fear we will have to move again before long. Mrs. Nelson says she finds it very difficult to get provisions.

March 8th. Tuesday. [1864]
The girl Mary came today, through all the rain, it made her quite sick for a day or two. Dr. Dean came to see her—

March 9th. [1864]
We blind folded Johnny the first day and he nursed, but it frightened him—

March 10th. [1864]
We can't coax Johnny to nurse—he won't do it.

March 13th. Sunday. [1864]
Johnny nursed at last today. The Capt. went out to Mr. Grant to spend the day. Maria McRorie spend the day and went to Church with me.

Tuesday March 15th. 1864.
They are exchanging all of our prisoners—

Poor Susan, Johnny's nurse left us today. I felt sorry for her.

Sunday 19th. [March, 1864]
Martha McRorie spent the day with me. In the afternoon I was taken sick with headache—the ladies went around to the square to see our returned prisoners. Johnny seem to enjoy it. I weaned my darling boy about the fifteenth & was taken sick at the same time.

Monday 21st. [March, 1864]
Johnny was taken sick—I believe from his teeth.

Wednesday. [March, 1864]
Johnny continued sick, and would not stay with anybody but me.

Friday 25th. [March, 1864]
Good Friday. I went to Church. When I returned I heard Tommy Williams was extremely ill—Mrs. Ann Williams and myself went to see him & found him very low and suffering agony apparently. The little fellow died on Saturday & was buried on Easter Sunday, a beautiful day it was.

My little darling has gotten quite well again.

Easter Sunday I went to Holy communion—In the evening Major Dashiel from Texas spent the evening with us.

April 30th. [1864]
A terrible accident occurred yesterday—The President's little boy Joe was killed—fell from up stairs down in the erea, a servant found the child first but already life had left him. His Mother and Father had walked out—

May 1st. 1864. Sunday.
We went to Church although it was raining. Father Huber preached about the blessed Virgin.

The President's child will be buried this evening.

May 12th. Thursday. [1864]
I left Richmond for Mecklenburg with Mr. R. Russell. I did not intend going to the country until June, but the great excitement in Richmond, and my being sick, determined my Husband to send me sooner.

Gen. Lee's Army had been fighting Grant's for about a week before I left, and is still fighting I believe.

The Yankees attempted to advance on R—by different directions. Beauregard whipped them or checked them near Drery Bluff—

Poor Gen. J. E. B. Stuart was wounded on the 11th. and died on the 12th May. I feel so much for his poor wife.

May 21st. [1864]
I have been at Mrs. Russell's for about ten days. I like it very much, they are all very kind to me. It is a sweet place—beautiful scenery all around. I have not heard from the Capt. but once since I came.

Johnny is getting along finely, I put short clothes on him on the 10th. May—he did not take any cold from it.

June 20th. [1864]
The Capt. came up to see us—having been sick he succeeded in getting a Furlough for six weeks.

June 25th. Saturday. [1864]
The Capt. had not been with me many days when he an Mr. Russell had to go down to Roanoke bridge to defend it. The Yankees having made a

raid advanced in large force to take it. The Capt. remained with the men during the fight, they repulsed the Yankees handsomely.

The Enemy came within ten or eleven miles of Mr. Russell's place. A great many of the neighbours went on the other side of the river for safety. We were not much alarmed.

The gentlemen returned on Sunday 26th all safe and sound. I felt uneasy about them although I never dreamed that they had an engagement. We have had intensely hot weather.

July 1st [1864]
A very warm day. We had a delightful little shower in the evening.

Johnny commenced to walk several days ago—and can say several words.

We have had a pleasant time at Mr. Russell's, all are very kind to us. We expect to go to Halifax on a little trip about Tuesday the 5th. I am anxious for our cousins to see Johnny.

July 4th. [1864]
My boy is a year old today, he can walk a little, and has said a few words. We spent his birthday at Mr. Russell's.

Oct. 5th. [1864]
They some fighting near Richmond about the 4th. & 5th. My Husband has gotten uneasy and determined to send me away again. Cousin John Brodnax has kindly invited me to his house in N. Carolina.

I concluded to send for Dr. Hughes, he prescribed for me. I was right in thinking I was more delicate than my friends imagined.

I started to Danville on the 12th. Oct.—exactly six months before I started for Meckenlenburg Co. I was very much opposed to leaving Richmond or rather my Husband, but he thought it the wisest course to pursue.

I started for Cousin John's on the 20th. October—I have been here ten today—I am very much pleased, I like the household very much—Cousin Bettie is one of the sweetest women I ever saw. I have two servants here, Susan and Mary—

Mary was taken sick on Sunday 6th so I concluded it was a good time to wean Johnnie. I made Easter, one of the servants here, stay in my room at night. I had not had near as much trouble as I anticipated. Johnny cries for me nearly all the time.

April 1st. 1865.
Saturday—A pleasant day. I exchanged nurses, I got Mary Heane from the sisters of Charity.

The 2ond. Sunday we went to Church, the Capt. went to Mr. Grant's farm afterwards. About two o'clock in the day Mr. Myers came around to Mrs. Nelson to inform the Capt. that Richmond was to be evacuated that afternoon.

Gen. Lee telegraphed Mr. Davis that the Yankees had broken through his lines in two different places and he feared would be compelled to give up Richmond & Petersburg.

My Husband did not return from the country until about 5 1/2, he left me about seven & half.

The President, Cabinet and all the officers belonging to the different departments started on the Cars for Danville, Va. expecting to remain some there and defend that country. My Husband sometimes advised me to go to North Carolina or some other part of the Confederacy, but I refused, believing it best to remain in Richmond, thinking it would be the easiest way I could reach my home.

I never spent two such nights in my life as I did the one of the evacuation and the one following, such fright, anxiety and dread I never before experienced. I felt sick for a week afterwards.

April 3rd. [1865]
The Yankees came into Richmond about nine O'clock in the morning. I moved up to Mr. Myer Myers the same day, they were all exceedingly kind to me, particularly Mr. Sol Myers. The Benjamins & The Crenshaws also invited me to stay with them. Mrs. Houseright stayed at the B. for some time.

Gen. Lee surrendered his army on the ninth of April, we southerners could scarcely believe it possible.

I heard from my dear Husband only once after we parted in Rich—he tells me to go home as soon as practicable. I started three weeks after the evacuation. Mr. G. T. Williams was my escort as far as New York, he was very attentive. We reached the city of N. York the very day that

President Lincoln's remains passed through the city, the place seemed gayer and more crowded than ever. I saw Mr. & Mrs. Roumage several times.

I remained in New Orleans two weeks waiting to see if they would allow me to go by Galveston,—through the kindness of Gen'l Wilcox and Judge Hancock I succeeded in getting permission.

I remained in Houston about ten days waiting for my brother to come for me. I stayed at the McGreal's, they were very kind to me.

Sunday June 4th. [1865]
I reached my dear home, my Mother of course was delighted to see me once more after a separation of nearly five years, she has given me a great many articles of clothing of hers & what belonged to my sweet sister.

June 8th. [1865]
A great many old friends have come to see me. I find my Uncle Tom very much altered, looks about fifteen years older than when I last saw him. Joe and Annette are staying out at the Ranch with Mr. & Mrs. Joe Magoffin.

I have not heard one word from my dear Husband, I trust he may soon get here.

June 18th. Sunday. [1865]
Joe, Annette and I went to the old church at ten o'clock. We had a good rain on our return home. Catarina & Carolina spent the day with us.

Poor Gen. Wilcox came to say farewell to me, he is about to start for Mexico with several other officers—they flee from their country on account of President Johnston proclamation—

My return to the Lone Star State dated June fourth 1865.

My Husband returned August 14th. '65.

Josephine was born Sept. 7th. 1865.

Poor Grandpapa died on the 6th. August.

4 Secession—Debate, Consequences, and Early Challenges

In early 1861, white Texans overwhelming supported secession. Sam Houston, who was then governor of Texas, was an important exception. Houston was a committed nationalist and believed that Texas was much stronger as part of the United States than as a state in the Confederate States of America. In September 1860, as the South began planning to leave the Union, he gave a famous speech in which he argued to white Texans that they were better off remaining a state within the United States. Houston, however, did not persuade his fellow Texans. In February 1861, they voted to overwhelming to leave the Union. The next month Houston resigned as governor. He was offered U.S. troops to fight secession in Texas, but he declined to fight against fellow Texans. Houston died in Huntsville in 1863.

Section 1. Governor Sam Houston Opposes Secession

Questions

1. Why does Sam Houston oppose secession?
2. Examine Sam Houston's feelings toward the Union. What makes him so loyal to the United States of America? Why, to him, is a unified national feeling much more important than secession?
3. For Sam Houston, what are the positive accomplishments of the United States, and why do these accomplishments make him so reluctant to leave the Union?
4. Why is Houston so unsympathetic to the calls for secession? For him, is the liberty of the

slaveholding South really under threat?

5. What, for Houston, are the dangers of secession for the slaveholding South?
6. How does Houston suggest that slaveholding Texans resist the efforts of the Lincoln administration to end slavery?

Document 1

Sam Houston's Anti-Secession Speech, September 22, 1860[1]

I had looked forward and with many pleasing anticipations to this occasion, as I always do to a meeting with my fellow-citizens, hoping that no untoward circumstance would arise to prevent my giving full utterance to my sentiments on the political topics of the day; but ill-health has overtaken me, and I have, against the advice of my physician, arisen from a sick-bed to make my apology for not being able to fill my appointment; but being here, I will endeavor to say a few words in behalf of the Union, and the necessity of union to preserve it, which I trust will not fall unheeded. The condition of the country is such, the dangers which beset it are so numerous, the foes of the Union so implacable and energetic, that no risk should be heeded by him who has a voice to raise in its behalf; and so long as I have strength to stand, I will peril even health in its cause.

I had felt an interest in this occasion, on many accounts. It is said a crisis is impending. The clamor of disunion is heard in the land. The safety of the Government is threatened; and it seemed to me that the time had come for a renewal of our vows of fidelity to the Constitution and to interchange, one with the other, sentiments of devotion to the whole country. I begin to feel that the issue really is upon us, which involves the perpetuity of the Government which we have received from our fathers. Were we to fail to pay our tributes to its worth, and to enlist in its defense, we would be unworthy longer to enjoy it.

It has been my misfortune to peril my all for the Union. So indissolubly connected is my life, my history, my hopes, my fortunes, with it,

1 Copyright in the Public Domain.

that when it falls, I would ask that with it might close my career, that I might not survive the destruction of the shrine that I had been taught to regard as holy and inviolate, since my boyhood. I have beheld it, the fairest fabric of Government God ever vouchsafed to man, more than a half century. May it never be my fate to stand sadly gazing on its ruins! To be deprived of it, after enjoying it so long, would be a calamity, such as no people yet have endured.

Upwards of forty-seven years ago, I enlisted, a mere boy, to sustain the National flag and in defense of a harassed frontier, now the abode of a dense civilization. Then disunion was never heard of ... It was anathematized by every patriot in the land, and the concocters of the scheme were branded as traitors. The peril I then underwent, in common with my fellow-soldiers, in behalf of the Union, would have been in vain, unless the patriotism of the nation had arisen against these disturbers of the public peace. With what heart could these gallant men again volunteer in defense of the Union, unless the Union could withstand the shock of treason and overturn the traitors? It did this; and when again, in 1836, I volunteered to aid in transplanting American liberty to this soil, it was with the belief that the Constitution and the Union were to be perpetual blessings to the human race,—that the success of the experiment of our fathers was beyond dispute, and that whether under the banner of the Lone Star or that many-starred banner of the Union, I could point to the land of Washington, Jefferson, and Jackson, as the land blest beyond all other lands, where freedom would be eternal and Union unbroken. It concerns me deeply, as it does every one here, that these bright anticipations should be realized; and that it should be continued not only the proudest nationality the world has ever produced, but the freest and the most perfect. I have seen it extend from the wilds of Tennessee, then a wilderness, across the Mississippi, achieve the annexation of Texas, scaling the Rocky Mountains in its onward march, sweeping the valleys of California, and laving its pioneer footsteps in the waves of the Pacific. I have seen this mighty progress, and it still remains free and independent. Power, wealth, expansion, victory, have followed in its path, and yet the aegis of the Union has been broad enough to encompass all. Is not this worth perpetuating? Will you exchange this for all the hazards, the anarchy and carnage of civil war? Do you believe that it will be dissevered and no shock felt in society? You are asked to plunge into a revolution;

but are you told how to get out of it? Not so; but it is to be a leap in the dark—a leap into an abyss, whose horrors would even fright the mad spirits of disunion who tempt you on....Have we not emerged from an infant's to a giant's strength? Have not empires been added to our domain, and States been created? All the blessings which they promised their posterity have been vouchsafed; and millions now enjoy them, who without this Union would to-day be oppressed and down-trodden in far-off foreign lands!

What is there that is free that we have not? Are our rights invaded and no Government ready to protect them? No! Are our institutions wrested from us and others foreign to our taste forced upon us? No! Is the right of free speech, a free press, or free suffrage taken from us? No! Has our property been taken from us and the Government failed to interpose when called upon? No, none of these! The rights of the States and the rights of individuals are still maintained. We have yet the Constitution, we have yet a judiciary, which has never been appealed to in vain—we have yet just laws and officers to administer them; and an army and navy, ready to maintain any and every constitutional right of the citizen. Whence then this clamor about disunion? Whence this cry of protection to property or disunion, when even the very loudest in the cry, declared under their Senatorial oaths, but a few months since, that no protection was necessary? Are we to sell reality for a phantom?

...How would these seceding States be received by foreign powers? If the question of their nationality could be settled (a difficult question, I can assure you, in forming treaties), what do you suppose would be stipulations to their recognition as powers of the earth? Is it reasonable to suppose that England, after starting this Abolition movement and fostering it, will form an alliance with the South to sustain slavery? No; but the stipulation to their recognition will be, the abolition of slavery. Sad will be the day for the institution of slavery, when the Union is dissolved, and with war at our very doors, we have to seek alliances with foreign powers. Its permanency, its security, are coequal with the permanency and the security of the Union under the Constitution.

When we are rent in twain, British Abolition, which in fanaticism and sacrificial spirit, far exceeds that of the North (for it has been willing to pay for its fanaticism, a thing the North never will do), will have none of the impediments in its path, now to be found. England will no longer fear the power of the mighty nation which twice has humbled her, and whose giant arm would, so long as we are united, be stretched forth to protect the weakest State, or the most obscure citizen. The State that secedes, when pressed by insidious arts of abolition emissaries, supported by foreign powers, when cursed by internal disorders and insurrections, can lay no claim to that national flag, which when now unfurled, ensures the respect of all nations and strikes terror to the hearts of those who would invade our rights. No! Standing armies must be kept—armies to keep down a servile population at home, and to meet the foe which at any moment may cross the border, bringing in their train ruin and desolation. Do you wish to exchange your present peaceful condition for the day of standing armies, when all history has proved that a standing army in time of peace is dangerous to liberty? Behold Cuba, with her 20,000 lazy troops, eating the substance of the people and ready at the beck of their masters to inflict some new oppression upon a helpless people; and yet, without a standing army, no State could maintain itself and keep down its servile population.

It is but natural that we all should desire the defeat of the Black Republican candidates. As Southern men, the fact that their party is based upon the one idea of opposition to our institutions, is enough to demand our efforts against them; but we have a broader, a more national cause of opposition to them. Their party is sectional. It is at war with those principles of equality and nationality upon which the Government is formed, and as much the foe of the Northern as of the Southern man. Its mission is to engender strife, to foster hatred between brethren, and to encourage the formation here of Southern sectional parties equally dangerous to Southern and Northern rights. The conservative energies of the country are called upon to take a stand now against the Northern sectional party, because its strength betokens success. Defeat and overthrow it, and the defeat and overthrow of Southern sectionalism is easy.

...I come not here to speak in behalf of a united South against Lincoln. I appeal to the nation. I ask not the defeat of sectionalism by sectionalism, but by nationality . . . The error has been that the South has met sectionalism by sectionalism. We want a Union basis, one broad enough to comprehend the good and true friends of the Constitution at the North. To hear Southern disunionists talk, you would think the majority of the Northern people were in this Black Republican party; but it is not so. They are in a minority, and it but needs a patriotic movement like that supported by the conservatives of Texas, to unite the divided opposition to that party there and overthrow it. Why, in New York, Pennsylvania, and New Jersey alone, the conservatives had a majority of over 250,000 at the last Presidential election, and in the entire North a majority of about 270,000." Because a minority at the North are inimical to us, shall we cut loose from the majority, or shall we not rather encourage the majority to unite and aid us? ... Hence I am ready to vote the Union ticket, and if all the candidates occupy this national ground, my vote may be transferred to either of them. This is the way to put Mr. Lincoln down. Put him down constitutionally, by rallying the conservative forces and sacrificing men for the sake of principles.

But if, through division in the ranks of those opposed to Mr. Lincoln, he should be elected, we have no excuse for dissolving the Union. The Union is worth more than Mr. Lincoln, and if the battle is to be fought for the Constitution, let us fight it in the Union and for the sake of the Union. With a majority of the people in favor of the Constitution, shall we desert the Government and leave it in the hands of the minority? A new obligation will be imposed upon us, to guard the Constitution and to see that no infraction of it is attempted or permitted. If Mr. Lincoln administers the Government in accordance with the Constitution, our rights must be respected. If he does not, the Constitution has provided a remedy.

No tyrant or usurper can ever invade our rights so long as we are united. Let Mr. Lincoln attempt it, and his party will scatter like chaff before the storm of popular indignation which will burst forth from one end of the country to the other. Secession or revolution will not be justified until legal and constitutional means of redress have been tried, and I can not believe that the time will ever come when these will prove inadequate.

If the people constitutionally elect a President, is the minority to resist him? Do they intend to carry that principle into their new Southern Confederacy? If they do, we can readily conceive how long it will last. They deem it patriotism now to overturn the Government.

Let them succeed, and in that class of patriots they will be able to outrival Mexico.

Section 2. Some Early Concerns for Confederate Texans

The following letters illustrate the uncertain environment Texans endured in the early days of the Civil War. As the Civil War began, Texas was vulnerable to external attack on several fronts. In addition, many citizens questioned Sam Houston's allegiance to the Confederate cause. In the early days of secession, anxious officials scrambled to achieve stability and security. The following letters address these critical concerns.

Questions

1. According to Clark, what measures had Texas taken to provide security for the Texas frontier and borders?
2. Why was Clark anxious to expedite the arrival of a Confederate regiment to bolster defenses in Texas?
3. What were his concerns about Sam Houston? After you read E. C. Wharton's letter and Houston's letter to Colonel Waite, analyze the validity of these concerns.

Document 1

April 4, 1861, Letter to Jefferson Davis from Edward Clark[2]

Executive Department
Austin, Tex., April 4, 1861

His Excellency Jefferson Davis,
President of the Confederate States:
Sir: This communication will be handed to you By General J. H. Rogers, who goes to your Government as the accredited agent of Texas. He is fully authorized for the purposes of his mission, which are to negotiate

2 Copyright in the Public Domain.

for the reception into the service of the Confederate States of the regiment of cavalry recently raised by Texas.

This regiment was authorized by an ordinance of the Convention of Texas for the purpose of defending our suffering frontier from the depredations of hostile Indians and the possible invasion of Mexican guerrillas. The provision was made during our transition state, before we had a right to expect the protection of your Government, and before you could have afforded us any security. It was an act of immediate, imperative necessity. Having 1,700 miles of frontier, with the ungoverned Mexicans on the west, who are our perpetual foes, we were forced to take some steps for immediate protection. Now, however, that we are under the guardianship of the Government of the Confederate States it is right that the defense of our frontier (which is its frontier) should not be assumed by this State, but should be sustained by that Government upon which devolves the military defense of the entire country.

It is more than probable that an effort will soon be made by the submission party of this State, with general Houston at its head, to convert Texas into an independent republic, and one of the most effective arguments will be that the Confederate States have supplied the place of the 2,800 United States troops formerly upon our frontier with only a single regiment and that Texas has at her own cost been forced to bring another regiment into the fields, and to bear the burden of its maintenance. The people of this State have been positively assured that their protection would be far more perfect under the Government of the Confederate States than it was under that old United States, and upon this reassurance they now rely. Hence I cannot too urgently press upon you the policy and equity of accepting the regiment of mounted volunteers which Texas has ordered out. Our protection properly devolves upon you, and if we receive it, Texas will not only be secured against a spirit of dissatisfaction and dissention with the Confederate States, but there will be given an eternal quietus to that spirit of opposition which is always grumbling in our midst.

Our situation in detail will be unfolded to you by General Rogers, who was one of the committee on public safety, and has familiarized himself with all the facts.

Very respectfully,
EDWARD CLARK

Document 2

Houston's problematic position, April 9, 1861. Letter from E. C. Wharton.[3]

"News" Office, Galveston Tuesday Morning, April 9, 1861

Dear Sir: I write in a hurry by Major Bickley, a brother of General Bickley, the head of the K.G.C. The major has had much to do with the working of secession in Western Texas, and can give you a good deal of news. General Austin has returned at his suggestion, as no time is to be lost.

I write to say that in case of hostilities we are totally unprotected here. There are a number of pieces of artillery here, brought from Brazos, but there is no powder, no military organization, no leader, no nothing. All our sea coast, and consequently all our ports and harbors, will be at the mercy of any small vessel of war that may choose to appear off Galveston, Indianola, &c., and dictate such terms as may please her commander. A vessel of war can come within two miles of our island, and we could be shelled without trouble.

Your Government should take instant steps to arm the Texas harbors. A good many people begin to ask why the other ports should be in defense and those of Texas not. The Convention did nothing for us in this respect, as they were thought it the duty of the Confederate Government to provide artillery and engineers and a commanding officer for the State, &c.

You can fancy our position if our trade with New Orleans were stopped suddenly by one of father Abraham's war steamers. We should have a military commander for the coast, with power to organize a corps

3 Copyright in the Public Domain.

of artillery and engineers; some columbiads, powder, &c. We have several hundred well-drilled men here, but they are not organized, and without that, would be inefficient.

Captain Talbot, of the steamship Mexico, informed us yesterday that he learned the day before from Captain Murray, of a steamship Fashion (chartered by the United States officers to take the United States troops from Indianola to the transport steamships outside), that he had been told to hold off, as he would not be needed until July. He seems to think that it was the intention to retain and concentrate the rest of the United States troops in Texas (some fifteen hundred) at or near Indianola.

We have published letters from Brownsville, Austin, and Washington that show it was Houston's design, in case his late appeal to the people took effect, to call on the United States troops to back him.

Respectfully,
E.C. Wharton

Document 3

Houston, March 29, 1861, letter to Colonel Waite declining U.S. troops to fight against secession[4]

Austin, March 29, 1861

Dear Sir:

I have received intelligence
that you have or will soon
receive orders to consantrate [sic]
United States troops under your
command at Indianola
in this State, to sustain me
in the exercise of my official
functions.

Allow me most respect-

4 Copyright in the Public Domain.

fully to decline any such assistance of the United States Government, and to most earnestly protest against the consentration [sic] of troops or fortifications in Texas; and request that you remove all such troops out of this State at the earliest day practicable, or at any rate, by all means take no actions towards a hostile movement till further orders by the Government at Washington City or particularly of Texas.

Thine
(signed) Sam Houston

To

Col Waite of
U.S. Army,
San Antonio,
Texas.

Section 3. Secession—Why Secede?

After Abraham Lincoln's election, Southern states began to secede from the Union. Each state submitted a declaration that listed its reasons for breaking away from the United States. Texas was no exception. Despite internal debate about the wisdom of secession and despite the disapproval of then-governor Sam Houston,

Texas voted to secede from the Union in February 1861. The following document contains the state's official reasons for that choice.

Questions

1. What major grievances were addressed in this document?
2. List some of the descriptive words included in this document. What attitudes do these words and images evoke?
3. In addition to the issue of protecting slavery, this document referred to the problem of defending Texas's southern border. According to the declaration, how did the federal government fail to protect Texas borders?
4. Review the third clause of the second section of the fourth article of the U.S. Constitution. How was this portion of the Constitution relevant in Texas's argument for secession?
5. What role did the issue of slavery play in the decision of the Texas secession convention to vote to leave the Union?

Document 1

Declaration of Causes: Austin, February 2, 1861[5]

A declaration of the causes which impel the State of Texas to secede from the Federal Union. (edited by R. Minten)

The government of the United States, by certain joint resolutions, bearing date the 1st day of March, in the year A.D. 1845, proposed to the Republic of Texas, then a free, sovereign and independent nation, the annexation of the latter to the former as one of the co-equal States thereof,

The people of Texas, by deputies in convention assembled, on the fourth day of July of the same year, assented to and accepted said proposals and formed a constitution for the proposed State, upon which on the 29th day of December in the same year, said State was formally admitted into the Confederated Union.

5 Copyright in the Public Domain.

Texas abandoned her separate national existence and consented to become one of the Confederated States to promote her welfare, insure domestic tranquility [sic] and secure more substantially the blessings of peace and liberty to her people. .. She was received as a commonwealth holding, maintaining and protecting the institution known as negro slavery—the servitude of the African to the white race within her limits—a relation that had existed from the first settlement of her wilderness by the white race, and which her people intended should exist in all future time. Her institutions and geographical position established the strongest ties between her and other slave-holding States of the confederacy. Those ties have been strengthened by association. But what has been the course of the government of the United States, and of the people and authorities of the non-slave-holding States, since our connection with them?

The controlling majority of the Federal Government, under various pretences and disguises, has so administered the same as to exclude the citizens of the Southern States, unless under odious and unconstitutional restrictions, from all the immense territory owned in common by all the States on the Pacific Ocean, for the avowed purpose of acquiring sufficient power in the common government to use it as a means of destroying the institutions of Texas and her sister slave-holding States.

By the disloyalty of the Northern States and their citizens and the imbecility of the Federal Government, infamous combinations of incendiaries and outlaws have been permitted in those States and the common territory of Kansas to trample upon the federal laws, to war upon the lives and property of Southern citizens in that territory, and finally, by violence and mob law, to usurp the possession of the same as exclusively the property of the Northern States.

The Federal Government, while but partially under the control of these our unnatural and sectional enemies, has for years almost entirely failed to protect the lives and property of the people of Texas against the Indian savages on our border, and more recently against the murderous forays of banditti from the neighboring territory of Mexico; and when our State government has expended large amounts for such purpose, the Federal Government has refused reimbursement therefor, thus rendering our condition more insecure and harrassing than it was during the existence of the Republic of Texas.

These and other wrongs we have patiently borne in the vain hope that a returning sense of justice and humanity would induce a different course of administration.

The States of Maine, Vermont, New Hampshire, Connecticut, Rhode Island, Massachusetts, New York, Pennsylvania, Ohio, Wisconsin, Michigan and Iowa, by solemn legislative enactments, have deliberately, directly or indirectly violated the 3rd clause of the 2nd section of the 4th article of the federal constitution, and laws passed in pursuance thereof; thereby annulling a material provision of the compact, designed by its framers to perpetuate amity between the members of the confederacy and to secure the rights of the slave-holdings States in their domestic institutions—a provision founded in justice and wisdom, and without the enforcement of which the compact fails to accomplish the object of its creation. Some of those States have imposed high fines and degrading penalties upon any of their citizens or officers who may carry out in good faith that provision of the compact, or the federal laws enacted in accordance therewith.

In all the non-slave-holding States, in violation of that good faith and comity which should exist between entirely distinct nations, the people have formed themselves into a great sectional party, now strong enough in numbers to control the affairs of each of those States, based upon the unnatural feeling of hostility to these Southern States and their beneficent and patriarchal system of African slavery, proclaiming the debasing doctrine of the equality of all men, irrespective of race or color—a doctrine at war with nature, in opposition to the experience of mankind, and in violation of the plainest revelations of the Divine Law. They demand the abolition of negro slavery throughout the confederacy, the recognition of political equality between the white and the negro races, and avow their determination to press on their crusade against us, so long as a negro slave remains in these States.

They have refused to vote appropriations for protecting Texas against ruthless savages, for the sole reason that she is a slave-holding State.

And, finally, by the combined sectional vote of the seventeen non-slave-holding States, they have elected as president and vice-president of the whole confederacy two men whose chief claims to such high positions are their approval of these long continued wrongs, and their pledges to continue them to the final consummation of these schemes for the ruin of the slave-holding States.

In view of these and many other facts, it is meet that our own views should be distinctly proclaimed.

We hold as undeniable truths that the governments of the various States, and of the confederacy itself, were established exclusively by the white race, for themselves and their posterity; that the African race had no agency in their establishment; that they were rightfully held and regarded as an inferior and dependent race, and in that condition only could their existence in this country be rendered beneficial or tolerable.

That in this free government all white men are and of right ought to be entitled to equal civil and political rights; that the servitude of the African race, as existing in these States, is mutually beneficial to both bond and free, and is abundantly authorized and justified by the experience of mankind, and the revealed will of the Almighty Creator, as recognized by all Christian nations; while the destruction of the existing relations between the two races, as advocated by our sectional enemies, would bring inevitable calamities upon both and desolation upon the fifteen slave-holding States.

By the secession of six of the slave-holding States, and the certainty that others will speedily do likewise, Texas has no alternative but to remain in an isolated connection with the North, or unite her destinies with the South.

For these and other reasons, solemnly asserting that the federal constitution has been violated and virtually abrogated by the several States named, seeing that the federal government is now passing under the control of our enemies to be diverted from the exalted objects of its creation to those of oppression and wrong, and realizing that our own State can no longer look for protection, but to God and her own sons—We the delegates of the people of Texas, in Convention assembled, have passed an ordinance dissolving all political connection with the government of the United States of America and the people thereof and confidently appeal to the intelligence and patriotism of the freemen of Texas to ratify the same at the ballot box, on the 23rd day of the present month.

Adopted in Convention on the 2nd day of Feby, in the year of our Lord one thousand eight hundred and sixty-one and of the independence of Texas the twenty-fifth.

5 Texas and the Civil War

Section 1. The Unionist Perspective

Pockets of Unionists existed within Texas throughout the Civil War. Many of these loyalists were citizens of German extraction. As the war dragged on, confrontations occurred that tested the allegiance of Texas residents—should they remain loyal to the state, which was part of the federal union, or to the new alliance with the Confederacy? Anthony M. Dignowity was a prominent Texas immigrant of Czech extraction. He entered Texas during the Mexican War, stayed to set up a lucrative doctor's practice, and gained notoriety by voicing abolitionist views. Because of his views, he often encountered threats and persecution; however, throughout the war, he remained vocal in his criticism of slavery and his support of free labor. In the following letter, Dignowity envisions the end of slavery in a prosperous, harmonious Texas. His views on free labor echoed those of most Lincoln Republicans. Dignowity, too, offers an idealistic version of free labor just as he assumes that freed slaves will be isolated in some undetermined area away from white society.

Questions

1. How did Dignowity visualize the future of freed slaves from Texas?
2. What did Dignowity see as the future economic structure of Texas?
3. Describe Dignowity's overall view of slavery.

4. Why was Dignowity, a Czech immigrant, an advocate for German immigrants in Texas?
5. Dignowity wrote of a "moral revolution." What would he see as the outcome of this revolution? Was that accomplished during Reconstruction?
6. What was Dignowity's view of Lincoln?

Document 1

December 24, 1861—Letter from Anthony M. Dignowity to the Honorable Senate and House of Representatives in Congress Assembled[1]

The memorialist, Anthony M. Dignowity respectfully represents: That himself and thousands of others, citizens of the United States, of German origin, having resided many years in the State of Texas, to which they were invited to settle, with the most solemn assurances held out to them that if not all, at least the larger portion of the State of Texas will be made a free State; that contrary to these promises a strong combination of men, whose avowed design was the extension and propagating of negro slavery, which is the great enemy of free labor, calculated to enrich a few at the expense of the many, this combination, growing more and more powerful, have, by various methods of oppression and tyranny, used every means, howsoever the most infamous and oppressive, to silence the just demands of your memorialist, which eventually resulted in the most stupendous conspiracy to overthrow and destroy the best government on earth. To this infamous crime your memorialist, together with thousands of loyal citizens of German origin, refused to become a party, were persecuted and hunted like malefactors, and in a great many instances, driven out of Texas, deprived of their hard-earned property, and being deprived of the legal rights of representation in your honorable bodies, no other method remains of making themselves heard only through this form of petition to lay their many wrongs and grievances before your honorable bodies, praying for justice and redress. Your memorialist

1 Copyright in the Public Domain.

would further draw the attention of Congress to the fact that at present near or about sixty-five thousand soldiers of German origin are in the field to sacrifice their lives if necessary, to uphold and restore the power of our common government over all the States and Territories of this Union. Your memorialist would respectfully submit to your collective wisdom and sense of right, not as a particular reward to us of German origin, but as a great policy of national economy, to direct the executive power so that the speedy reconquest of Texas may be affected, and to convert said State into a free State. To affect this object, it would be flattering and congenial to the feelings of all the citizens of German origin if part of that army composed of the German citizen soldiers would be employed to bring freedom and deliverance from the most despotic bondage suffered by thousands of loyal citizens still remaining on the soil of Texas. Your memorialist would hazard his opinion suggestive to carry out such measures into effect; first, the following plan: An army of ten thousand strong could be landed either at Corpus Christi or at Indianola, there to take a position and await the co-operation of an army advance, which should be made from the borders of Kansas, of at least twenty-five thousand strong, which army should advance through the Indian country, would overawe those tribes now partially in rebellion, and will bring them back to their allegiance to the United States; then advancing along the lines of the military posts into Texas. And there form a junction with the first army of ten thousand strong, already occupying the sea-coast. This combined force, if desirable, could be strongly strengthened from the loyal citizens of Texas, and would soon make short work of the rebellion in that State, and, if necessary, its force could turned either against Louisiana or Arkansas; then a wise and equitable measure of negro emancipation could be put in force, indemnifying those *few* loyal owners, and, of course, confiscating all property of the rebels of every kind; then to remove said negroes either to Florida or some other locality which may have been selected for such purpose to colonize them. The Texas, freed from this blasting incubus would and should be open to German and other free-soil immigrants. This, in the view of your memorialist, would form a great plan of political economy, and would present incalculable advantages, and will be pregnant with immense results. Texas, if once open to free-labor, could produce all the cotton needed in the world—not only that staple, but a large portion of sugar, rice, tobacco, hemp; also small grains of every kind; the best and abundant crops of the finest wool; nay, the geniality and salubrity of the climate is adapted to the South American llama, sheep, alpaca, and hundreds, nay, thousands, other branches of industry; the facilities for railroads; its facilities for manufacturing of every kind, in localities of unrivaled water-power, nay, it contains within itself the germ of a large empire. There is another item that will not escape your legislative wisdom. Texas is still an unappropriated public domain, consisting of over one hundred millions of acres of land. This, as a matter of course, is forfeited by the rebellion to the federal government. Would it not be wise and just to grant bounty warrants to the soldiers from this great domain, with a view to its distribution and settlement with free laborers? Let us again turn from this great prospective future to those sad realities of the present. I would crave your attention and indulgence to state my individual views on this tremendous crisis. I view this as a necessary sequel of the great revolution of the past century, and I shall be satisfied if its duration shall not exceed the first struggle, the last or present one being the more important *moral revolution*. That it will be accomplished thoroughly I entertain not the least doubts whatsoever. When it will be accomplished there will not remain on this continent one single foot of soil subject to monarchical rule, neither will there remain on this continent one single human being owned by others as a slave. This great work or mission the American people are bound and are destined to accomplish—yes, the complete abolishment of the African slave trade, when there shall remain no market for human beings. War with foreign powers is unavoidable, whatsoever diplomacy will attempt to the contrary; but who fears the result? This great nation is preparing for all emergencies, and will be amply able to meet them. God in his wisdom has established immutable laws of progress, and, according to those laws, onward and forward is our motto. In conclusion, I would take the liberty to admonish all that a unity of purpose is essential, nay, necessary. Our experience will be our great teacher. Humanity demands that the greatest results shall be obtained with the smallest sacrifices of human life. The French revolution and the massacres of St. Domingo should admonish us to moderation and wisdom. Our John Browns must not be permitted to act contrary to the wisdom of our present ruler. He is the one selected under Divine Providence by the suffrages of his countrymen to occupy the highest trust ever conferred on any man. From the judgment I have formed of his character, I believe his greatest errors will be those committed on the side of humanity. Individually I consider him to fill the right place at the right time. All have the right to advise in courtesy, but only one must direct, or anarchy and indiscriminate slaughter will soon be the result. Our guide must be binding on our acts. Wisdom, justice, freedom, humanity, are universal principles, and must be applied universally.

Respectfully submitted by
Anthony M. Dignowity
of San Antonio, Texas,

on behalf of himself and thousands of loyal citizens of Texas, particularly of German origin.

Section 2. Border Security

F. R. Lubbock served as governor of Texas from 1861 to 1863. In this letter to Confederate President Jefferson Davis, Lubbock asked that Davis allow Texas troops to guard Texas borders and protect Texans from invasion. Another factor that troubled Lubbock was the frequency of Indian attacks—something that other Confederate states rarely experienced.

Questions

1. According to Lubbock, why was guarding the Texas borders crucial?
2. What challenges did being located on the periphery of the Confederate States of America bring to the state?
3. In addition to invasion by the Union army, Texans had to guard against Indian attacks. How might this have affected the use of military personnel in Texas?
4. Do Lubbock's concerns seem legitimate? Why or why not?

Document 1

Executive Department, Austin, Nov 13, 1862[2]

My dear sir,

I have the honor to acknowledge the receipt of your communication bearing date 12th Sept and directed to myself and others. For the kind expressions and the manifest interest entertained by you on behalf of the states West of the Miss please receive my acknowledgements –
I am also in receipt of letters from Messrs. Sexton and Gray members of Congress from our state of a very satisfactory character. They both inform me that from conversations with you, they were led to believe you would for the present require no more men to leave Texas. Let me assure Your Excellency that Texas is almost denuded of her best fighting men. We have over 50 Regts in the Confederate service very few of which are in the state. We are also very badly off for arms. Our men took with them the best arms they could contest. We have an immense frontier and sea country to look after both of which, is now seriously threatened with invasion. May I hope under the circumstances that you will for the present suspend the enforcement

of the new conscript law within our state. The Commanding Genl has called upon me for for 2000 state troops for the defense of the state and if the new for a short period I am busily

2 Copyright in the Public Domain.

engaged raising them, should [?]
the new laws be imposed I do not believe
I can get them.There is a feverish anxiety
pervading the Public Mind as to what may happen
here this winter. We appear to the allegedly being assaulted
on the coast by the enemies Gun Boats and
marauding parties; if nothing more formidable
invasion is expected on our Northern Border
When recently great outrages here have been
committed by Indians and Jay Hawkes,
as also the discovery of many from Territory.
Many believe that we will be invaded
from the West; under these circumstances
our People are really uneasy. They all
will leave home poorly provided [?][?]
with arms and ammunition; hence the
great reluctance to see any more men
leave the state at this time.I have at all times
and on all occasions assisted in sending
men out of the State to scenes of war
action and I dislike now to
admit that we should send no more.

I am however of the opinion
that the [?] men in Texas should be
permitted to remain here until next
Spring, and if by that time necessity should
require Texas to furnish an additional
number I feel safe in saying that her
people will be ready to respond.The permitting of so many new
organizations since the passage of the Conscription
law has done much harm and I assure
you that unless Regts are consolidated
the old ones can never be filled up.
I of course only speak for Texas, I know not
how it is in other localities.I am clearly of

the opinion that the Old Regiments that have seen
so much hard service and reflected so
much on themselves and performed
such gallant deeds for the country
should be fostered cherished and cared
for. Those veterans should be kept together
and their identity preserved even if it
be at the expense of the late organizations.
Can you not spare us a
few thousand arms for this state. If
we could get back the old rifles and shot
guns that have been taken off by our men
and which [?] have been laid aside
for men appears this we would
feel better able to defend our state.
If I could be assured of any
firearms I would send an agent
to attend to their transportation.
Will you not send an order
to the Commanding Genl suspending the
late act for the present within the
state of Texas.Let me hope to hear
from you soon.

With Sentimental assurances
of my high regard and esteem
I am your Excellent
friend

F.R. Lubbock

Section 3. Runaway Slave Advertisements in Wartime Texas Newspapers

Slaves ran away for many reasons. Slavery was very cruel, and the life of the slave was not a happy one. Many slaves were beaten and tortured. Often, slave families were torn apart when the members were sold to different owners. Some slaves did not have enough to eat, warm clothes, or a decent place to live. Sometimes slaves ran away because they were going to be sold. Texas was unique in that runaway slaves ran south toward Mexico. Mexico had abolished slavery in 1829, and once slaves crossed the Rio Grande they were free under Mexican law. During the Civil War, a number of slaves were "refugeed" into Texas from regions of nearby states, especially Louisiana, occupied by the Union Army. Some historians argue that by 1865, the year Texas slaves were emancipated, there were up to 250,000 slaves in the Lone Star State. The runaway slave advertisements below are just a small sampling of many that appeared in Texas before and during the Civil War.

Questions

1. How are slaves described in these advertisements?
2. Do these advertisements indicate whether or not slaves were able to create families?
3. What do these advertisements indicate about the number of skills possessed by slaves in Texas?
4. Do these advertisements indicate an education level among Texas slaves?
5. What does Document 3 indicate about how the Confederate government utilized slaves during the Civil War?
6. What are the various physical attributes given the runaway slaves in this set of documents?
7. How much were slave owners willing to pay for the capture of their runaway slaves?

Document 1

The Washington Telegraph and McKinney Messenger, *September 28, 1861*[3]

RANAWAY On Friday morning the 27th, from my house in Clarksville, the negro man, BOB, who calls himself Robt. Allison—a dark mulatto with grey eyes, about 43 years old; one of his ears cropped off, the upper part; has a long forehead, and his hair somewhat grey in front.—He is about five feet nine inches high and will weigh about 150 pounds. He is a barber by trade, raised in Washington D. C., and has the manners of a well raised city negro. I will give a liberal reward for the apprehension and delivery of said negro to me, or confinement in Jail so that I can get him. W. P. DICKSON.

Document 2

The Houston Tri-Weekly Telegraph, *June 12, 1863*

RANAWAY—My negro boy GEORGE, rather low stature with a scar on the back part of his neck, whiskers on his chin and upper lip, about 34 years old; Another boy, SAM, about 20 years old, very straight, rather light color; And another one, ALFORD, about 20 or 21 years old, about 5 feet 7 1/2 inches high, light color. They were brought from Mississippi about one week ago. Perhaps they will give the name of Van Heusen when taken up, as I brought them over. A liberal reward will be paid for the delivery of them in any jail where I can get them. W. P. ENGLISH. Houston.

3 Documents 1-11 from Section 3 are all copyright in the Public Domain. They were accessed from the Texas Runaway Slave Project (TRSP), East Texas Research Center, Stephen F. Austin State University.

The Houston Tri-Weekly Telegraph, *December 9, 1863*

Document 3

Notice to Owners of Negroes. Headquarters, Labor Bureau, Houston, December 7th, 1863. THE frequent escape of Negroes from the different Departments to which they have been assigned to labor, renders it imperatively necessary for some course to be adopted to prevent so scurious and growing an evil. The injury to the service resulting from the loss of this labor at a time, often when most required, and the apparent reluctance upon the part of the owners to return their negroes, who have runaway from Government service, compels the adoption of the following stringent rule in reference to the matter. The owners or agents of negroes obtained for the Government service, either by the consent of the owners or by impressment, are hereby notified that when said negroes shall leave the Department to which they have been assigned to labor, and returning to their owners or agents, unless regularly discharged in writing by the proper officer, they are directed at once to return them to the Department from which they escaped; upon failure to comply with this order, double the number escaping will be required, and the officers of Bureau will be directed to impress the same. This rule will apply to all negroes that have been collected and runaway since the last call made, September 9th, 1863. By command of Major General J. B. MAGRUDER. T. C. Armstrong, Captain and Chief Labor Bureau. December 9, 1863

The Bellville Countryman, *June 21, 1864*

Document 4

COMMITTED. To the jail of Austin county on the 15th inst two negro slaves: one a man named Tom, about 55 years of age, very black about five feet high, head considerably gray: the other a woman named Sally, about 35 years old, very smal and black and sickly. They claim to be man and wife, and say they belong to Housen Thompson of Louisiana, and that he was running them to Columbia, Texas. They are very ignorant, and don't appear to know much about where they belong. The owner will prove them away or they will be disposed of according to law. Bellville April 21st 1864. CHARLES MANOR. Act'g Jailor.

Document 5

The Houston Weekly Telegraph, *March 8, 1864*

$150 REWARD.—Ranaway from Eagle Lake, February 24, 1864, three negroes as follows: Bob—5 feet 8 or 10 inches high, very black; Tolbert—copper colored, 5 feet 8 or 10 inches high; Edmund—5 feet 10 inches high, black. They will claim to belong to Louis Darobry, of Caddo Parish, Louisiana, and will endeavor to make their way back to Shreveport, crossing the Brazos probably at Washington, and then to Crockett and Henderson. They do not know any other road. I will pay the above reward for said negroes, if sent to me at Eagle Lake, or lodged in any jail and information sent to me on Eagle Lake. March 4- LORENZO DOWNING

Document 6

The Texas Republican, *Marshall, Texas, February 1, 1862*

The *Texas Republican*, Marshall, Texas, February 1, 1862

STOLEN. I HAVE not seen or heard from my negro man REUBEN since Wednesday last, very early in the morning. I have no doubt that he was enticed away by a thief, under the pretense of taking him to a free State. He may be with the thief, or traveling alone with a pass. I will pay a reasonable reward for his delivery to me in Marshall, Texas. He is about twenty-eight years of age, medium size and height, very black, a heavy suit of hair, and thin beard. He was raised in a hotel, has been a waiter in one in Jackson, Mississippi, in Shreveport, Louisiana, in Marshall and Jefferson, Texas. He is sprightly, intelligent, and very much addicted to lying. He has remarkably small eyes. DUDLEY S. JENNINGS. February 1, 1862

Document 7

The Texas Almanac, *January 29, 1863*

Description

NOTICE. RANAWAY from the subscribers, on Monday night 20th inst., a negro man, named Charles, of black complexion, about 5 feet 6 inches high, well built, aged 34 years. Also, his wife, Jane, a woman about 16 years of age, a bright mulatto, with yellow eyes, about 5 feet 6 inches high, tolerably slim. The boy, Charles, when he left, was riding a brown mare, with a blaze in her face, about 14 1/2 hands high, branded [B] R and D B, with one white foot. It is supposed his wife, Jane, is riding a bay horse (stallion), with a star in his forehead, shod all round. $300 REWARD! We will pay three hundred dollars to any person who will apprehend and deliver the above named negroes to us, eight miles east of Cameron, Milam County, Texas. We will also give the mare the boy Charles is riding, if taken with them. She is worth $150. It is supposed the above negroes are trying to get to Mexico. DANIEL COLLINS, January 29-1t JOHN BEAL

Document 8

Henderson Times, *August 19, 1863*

Description

$250 Reward. I will pay the above reward, of $250, for the delivery to me at Kickapoo, Anderson county, Texas or lodged in any jail so that I may get the following negroes, viz: A negro man about thrity-five or forty years old, by the name of Rich; dark complexion, about 5 feed 8 inches high, with a scar over, I think his right eye.–Also, his wife, Kittie, about 25 years old, copper color, medium size rather stammers in her speech, and speaks rather short. They left my place on the night of the 30th of July, 1863. I will pay for each negro $100 as above mentioned. J.B. Miller.

Document 9

The Houston Weekly Telegraph, *January* 7, *1861*

$25 REWARD.—The above reward will be paid for the delivery of my girl Lucy, who run away from Houston December 10; said girl is about 35 years old, bright mulatto, large form, and weighs about 170 or 180 pounds, with scars on her arm as if she had beenburned, swaggers when she walks, and is rather smart. Said girl was shipped by H. & T. C. R. R., to care of Mr. J. B. Gallaher, at Houston, and delivered to him on the date above named, and by permission was allowed to go across the street, and has not since been heard from. I will give the above reward for the apprehension of said girl, if taken out of Harris county, and delivered to Messrs Strother & Stone, Galveston; or $10 if taken in Harris County., and delivered to Mr. J. B. Gallaher, Houston; and if induced to runaway by a white man I will give $50 for his apprehension. G. W. STROTHER. Houston, January 7,1861

Document 10

The Houston Weekly Telegraph, *January 14, 1862*

RUNAWAY. $50 REWARD.— I will pay the above reward for the apprehension and delivery to me, or any jail, so I can get him, of my mulatto boy ALFRED. Said boy ran away from me, in Houston, on Sunday night, 12th inst. He has Mexican features, curly hair, hump shoulders, light beard, 5 feet 2 inches in height, weighs about 145 pounds, has lash marks on his back, speaks French and English and possibly Spanish. He can be recognized in Houston by Peter the Barber. My address is Washington, St. Landry,Louisiana, or Houston, Texas. ACTHEON CARRIERE. Houston, January 14, 1862.

Document 11

The Houston Tri-Weekly Telegraph, *September 11, 1863*

$500 REWARD.—Ranaway from James A. Hardin, near Jamestown, Smith Co., Texas, the 29th of July, 1863, a negro girl, Ellen, about 18 years old, nearly black, about 5 feet 5 inches high, her toes are about half as long as her big toes, and look like they were cut off; also she was badly burned when about eight years old, and left scars on each side of her legs, and I think on her back also. I have good reason to believe that she has been sent or taken off. If so, I will give the above reward for her and the thieflodged in Tyler jail, with the proper evidence to convict. If she has not been taken off, I will give a liberal reward for the said negro, delivered at my house one and a half miles north of Jamestown. JAMES A. HARDIN.

Section 4. The Biegel Resolution

The Biegel Settlement was a German-speaking immigrant community located between LaGrange and Columbus, Texas. In February of 1861, Fayette County voted on whether to secede from the Union. Many German-speaking immigrants did not support secession, and Fayette County voted not to secede by a 626 to 580 count. While a number of German-speaking Texans in this area of Central Texas served willingly in the Confederate Army, the vote against secession created a strong distrust among the German community by Confederate Army and State of Texas officials. These Confederate authorities feared many Germans in Texas were disloyal to the Southern effort.

Many German-speaking Texans in the LaGrange area were deeply angered when they were required to join the Confederate Army for three months. On January 4, 1863, a secret meeting was held in the Biegel Settlement and a letter was sent to the ranking Confederate officer in La Grange, Brigadier General William G. Webb, formerly a local lawyer. The letter outlined the resident's reasons for protesting the draft. The major objection was the increase in the poverty level for the farmer's families should they have to leave the farms. Five men stating that they represented about 120 citizens signed the letter. This was a very bold and potentially dangerous statement in a time of war.

The Confederacy reacted by declaring a state of martial law in Fayette County. The Governor of Texas, Francis Lubbock, immediately traveled to La Grange and met with the dissidents. The Governor gave a very plain, positive talk to them and extracted a promise of enlistment from a majority of the protesters. Lubbock's persuasive speech and the artillery piece belonging to the Confederate Cavalry Brigade that backed him up quieted things down. In addition, as the documents below indicate, Confederate officials did not hesitate to use strong army tactics against German-speaking civilians to force men to serve in the Confederate Army.

Questions

1. From your reading in the primary documents, how alarmed were Confederate authorities by the deep reluctance of many German-speaking residents near La Grange to serve in the Confederate Army? How seriously did they take this resistance on the part of these farmers?
2. In your opinion, did Confederate authorities overreact to this refusal of these farmers to join the Confederate Army?
3. Did Confederate authorities have the right to force male Texans, even those who did not support the war, to join the Confederate Army? Why or why not?
4. After reading these documents, do you believe the farmers that signed the so-called Biegel Resolution were a threat to the Confederacy?
5. Why did these farmers resist being forced into the Army? Does their resistance seem reasonable to you?
6. From your reading of these documents, were many of the farmers who signed the Biegel Resolution forced to fight with the Confederate Army?

Document 1

Austin, January 3, 1863, Austin, STATE OF TEXAS, ADJT. AND INSP. GENERAL'S OFFICE to Major A. G. DICKINSON to J. Y. DASHIELL, Adjutant and Inspector General[4]

MAJOR: In reply to your favor of 29th ultimo I am directed by the Governor to state that he construed the language of the general's communication of date of 20th December ultimo, to wit -

I have to request that you will call out at once all the militia which the State can possibly arm and cause them to rendezvous at Harrisburg to be another and distinct requisition from that of Brigadier General P. O. Hebert, of date November 8, 1862, which is as follows:

I have the honor to call upon you for not less than 5,000 militia soldiers, to serve for three months, unless sooner discharged.

He now understands from your communication of the 29th of December ultimo that the general commanding makes no call at this time for State troops, but that his communication of 20th December referred to the speedy concentration of the troops called out under the requisition of General Hebert at Houston.

I am pleased to inform you that by General Orders, No. 27, from this office, companies as soon as organized are ordered to report to you at the earliest practicable moment.

Very respectfully, your obedient servant,

ENROLLING OFFICE OF AUSTIN COUNTY,

4 Copyright in the Public Domain.

Document 2

Industry, January 3, 1863. A. J. BELL, Enrolling Officer Western District Austin County to Major J. P. FLEWELLEN, Superintendent of Conscripts, Austin, Tex.[5]

SIR: In addition to what I have heretofore reported, of date November 28, 1862, and December 25, 1862, I have the honor in this connection to further report that the Germans of my district and of the adjoining counties are in a state of open rebellion to our Government. They are holding meetings almost every day, and held a large meeting, consisting of about 600 persons, on the 31st of December, 1862, in Shelby Prairie, the upper portion of this county, and organized by calling Mr. C. Senman to the chair, and appointed a committee to draught resolution expressive of the sense of the meeting; whereupon the committee recommended that the following resolutions be adopted:

That the chair appoint one man in each beat to return home and call their men together, and then organize instanter into companies of infantry and cavalry, which has been done by electing captains and appointing specified times of drilling, which they have begun already; also keeping a picket guard mounted and armed, to be ready to communicate information to the officers in command.

Said meeting was represented by five counties, to wit: Austin, Washington, Fayette, Lavaca, and Colorado. They were called first by counties. Delegates answered to their names. Then they were called by beats. The following-names persons were present and delivered speeches in said meeting, all of whom were in favor of resistance to the Government and opposed to going into the service in any way: Fr. Mittanck, of New Ulm; F. Hanbold, of New Ulm;—Hildebrand, of Biegel settlement, Fayette County; H. Zulauf, of New Ulm;—Suliger, of Industry; F. W. Dorbritz, of New Ulm; C. Rungo, of New Ulm;—Helams, sr., of Roeder's Mill, Austin County;—Lewis, of La Grange, Fayette County (an American).

There was a draft held here about the 23rd of December in response to the Governor's proclamation for men. Quite a number of them were

5 Copyright in the Public Domain.

drafted and a great many were conscripts. These two combined have increased the rebellion to this pitch. The drafted men have continued to refuse to be sworn into the State service on the day appointed by the captain of Industry for the drafted men to be sworn into the service. He was assaulted and driven from the place appointed by him for said purpose; also a friend of his was actually mobbed, by being beaten with sticks, iron bars, & c.

Therefore, sir, I deem it to be my duty to ask for assistance again. Not less than one full regiment of cavalry, to be well mounted, armed, and supplied with subsistence to maintain them while so engaged, will do any good, but would meet with defeat. If there is a force sufficient to vindicate the majesty of the law at once it can be quelled without much bloodshed on our part, but if allowed to remain and mature would require a much greater sacrifice of life and property than if crushed out now at the beginning.

All of which is respectfully submitted.

HDQRS. TWENTY-SECOND BRIGADE TEXAS STATE TROOPS, La Grange, Tex., January 4, 1863[6]

Document 3

WILLIAM G. WEBB, Brigadier-General, Second Brigade Texas State Troops to Major A. G. DICKINSON, Assistant Adjutant-General, & c., Houston, Tex.:

MAJOR: I feel it my duty through you to lay before Major-General Magruder the following matters; and this is rendered the more necessary on account of the delay that must necessarily result in his hearing from the Governor, to whom last night I sent an express, and our militia laws are so faulty as not to concede authority to any one except the Governor to call out the State troops; yet should an emergency make it absolutely necessary I should assume the responsibility to do so. For several days expresses have come to me from various directions, at first giving mere rumors, but last evening more definite information. Dr. G. B. Robson came in last evening, having been sent by a number of very respectable

6 Copyright in the Public Domain.

citizens living in this county some 18 miles from here, bringing me the information that on last Wednesday from 500 to 700 men met at Roeder's Mill, just over the line of this county, in Austin County, and that they determined to resist the draft and conscription to the last extremity; that as soon as the drafted men are ordered out they mean to assemble and resist it; the the meeting was addressed by Germans and Americans; that they are organized and have their officers elected, and they mean to stir up insurrection with all of its horrors in case of conflict, and that six counties were represented. Dr. Robson states that this information was obtained from men who were at the meeting and that it is reliable. Dr. Robson is one of our most prominent citizens.

I also have reliable information that on last Tuesday night large numbers of armed men were seen to go from this (Austin) and Colorado Counties toward Roeder's Mill; one party was headed by an American and passed in the night. On Wednesday morning some 75 men, mostly armed, from this county passed through Fayetteville, a little town in this county 12 miles from here, and reported that they were going to Frelsburg, in Colorado County, but were watched and seen to leave the Frelsburg road and to take the road to Roeder's Mill.

A German, a true man, came to see me yesterday, and stated he wished to communicate something to me, but that he would not do so unless I promised to keep his name secret, and upon my doing so he told me that on Thursday the Germans of his neighborhood had met at the house of a drafted man, and there organized into a company and elected their officers to resist being taken off as drafted men, and also to resist conscription, and that they had threatened every German with destruction who would not join them; that they intended to wait until an attempt was made to force the men off, and then they would assemble and resist to the death.

Two other gentlemen of respectability (W. W. Wade and P. Clawson, of Fayetteville) came to me about midnight Friday night, and reported to me that this meeting detailed by this German was held, and that every movement indicated resistance; also that a German blacksmith in Fayetteville was discovered to be secretly making spear-heads; also that these men had in the last few weeks provided themselves with ammunition.

I also have information of three other meetings of Germans having been held in other and different neighborhoods in this county, all secret, and also of other meetings being appointed for to-day (Sunday) and Monday.

We have a large German population in this county, and in Colorado, Austin, and Washington Counties. Many of them are true men, and if we never had had a traitor American nearly all would have been, and the seeds of disaffection have been sown by native Americans, and they now have natives colleague with the disloyal among them. These secret meetings have been holding for months, but until lately have not attracted much attention. For some two weeks past, however, my attention has been frequently called to them, and I have labored incessantly to keep down the hot-headed men upon our side, in order that we might get into the design, and also to prevent anything being done which would precipitate a civil war and place us in the aggressive. I have, however, had true men on the alert, obtaining all the information possible, but they have been so cautious that this has been very difficult, and a German who was a secessionist was kicked out of one of the meetings, it is rumored, and charged with being a spy.

In times of public excitement it is most difficult to cull out the truth from exaggerated rumor, and while I would have our distinguished commander informed of these matters I would not be instrumental in stirring up unnecessary excitement. It has been because of the true men of this county knowing of the disaffected element among us that they have declined to volunteer, being unwilling to leave their families at home and they away, and also determined to make an issue with the disloyal by compelling them to meet the draft. I feel satisfied that we have true men enough among us to overcome the disloyal in case of an outbreak, but they have not the arms, having given them to those gone into the Army, while most of those believed to be disloyal are well armed.

Again, if civil war really is intended, and we were even well armed, we are very much scattered and surrounded by those who are suspected, and to attempt to assemble from the different neighborhoods would but give the disloyal the same opportunity, and the families of the true men be left defenseless.

I received an order from the Governor through the Adjutant-General to send forward the three-months' men to Houston as fast as companies could be organized, but in view of the fact that the draft is not yet made in all the counties, and particularly in view of the threat of resistance whenever an attempt should be made to force off the drafted men, and to give us time to prepare, I have issued orders, fixing Monday, the 12th of this month, for the time of assembling at Columbus. This postponement will perhaps delay a conflict, and enable us to get ready, and probably prevent it altogether.

With perfect deference to our able chieftain I most respectfully suggest that if a regiment of cavalry could be sent to the disaffected region it would overawe the disaffected and prevent an outbreak, if any is intended. Perhaps even a less number would do. If this were done under cover of forming an encampment to obtain supplies it would allay suspicion, and the drafted men would see the necessity of obeying the call, and all perhaps pass off quietly.

From all I can learn the greatest disaffection is about New Ulm and Industry, in Austin County, and Round Top and Fayetteville, in this county. Neither of these places is more than 10 or 12 miles apart. If a command of cavalry were placed in Fayetteville it would be convenient to all the other points, and could act according to circumstances. Fayetteville is about 18 miles from Alleyton, the head of the railroad, and there is plenty of corn in the neighborhood.

I have hesitated to address you because I know that the Governor is the proper officer for me to apply to, and I must make the great desire I have to prevent a conflict between our own citizens my excuse for the course taken.

If my paper and the manner in which I have written on it be against regulations let the scarcity of the article be my excuse.

P. S.–A gentleman has just come to me in haste to inform me of another meeting of Germans on yesterday on the west side of the Colorado River, in a German neighborhood, at which there were over 100 men present, and a German woman stated that their object was to resist the draft.

The Biegel Resolution[7]

At a public meeting held by the citizens in Biegel Settlement, Fayette County, Texas, on January 4, 1863, the following declaration was adopted as an expression of the sentiments of said meeting:

The measures taken by the Government to protect this State against invasion are so far-reaching and serious in their consequences that they fill our minds with dread and apprehension.

The past has already taught us how regardlessly the Government as the county authorities have treated the families of those who have taken the field. We have been told that they would be cared for, and what up to this timc has been done? They were furnished with small sums of paper money, which is almost worthless, and which has been refused by men for whose sake this war and its calamities were originated.

Last year we made tolerably good crops; the prospect for the next is not very encouraging, and we cannot look forward with indifference upon starvation, which we apprehend for our wives and children.

Although it has been said that we will not be needed for more than three months, the time for planting will then be over and our children may go begging, for the small pay which we are to receive for our services is insufficient to purchase bread for our families and pay for it. We and our families are almost destitute of clothing, and have no means of getting enough to protect us even imperfectly against the cold, from which cause sickness and epidemics result, as has been experienced in the Army, where more men have fallen victims of disease than by the sword of the enemy.

Last autumn we applied to procure cloth from the penitentiary, but up to this time we have not been able to obtain any, whereas negro-holders, whom we could name, can get such things and fetch them home. For these reasons we sympathize with all the unfortunate who have to provide for their own maintenance, and hope that our authorities will look upon us as men and not as chattels. With what spirit and what courage can we so situated fight, and that, moreover, for principles so far removed from us?

---

7 Copyright in the Public Domain.

Besides the duty of defending one's country there is a higher and more sacred one–the duty of maintaining the families. What benefit is there in preserving the country while the families and inhabitants of the same, nay, even the Army, are bound to perish in misery and starvation?

In view of the foregoing we take the liberty hereby jointly to declare that unless the Army and we obtain a guarantee that our families will be protected, not only against misery and starvation, but also against vexations from itinerant bands, we shall not be able to answer the call, and the consequences must be attributed to those who caused them.

Furthermore, we decline taking the army oath (as prescribed) to the Confederate States, as we know of no law which compels Texas troops, who are designed for this State, to take the same.

It is the unanimous wish of those assembled in this meeting to apply to Brigadier General W. G. Webb to use all of his influence to the effect that the men now drafted for militia service be permitted to stay at home until they have finished planting.

By authorization and in the name of about one hundred and twenty citizens.

C. AMBERG.
H. BAUCH.
R. HILDEBRAND.
H. KRALE.
H. HASSE.

I do hereby certify the above and foregoing to be a true and correct copy of the original (translation).

JAMES PAUL,
Private Secretary.

Document 5

HDQRS. TWENTY-SECOND BRIGADE TEXAS STATE TROOPS, Columbus, Tex., January 12, 1863. WILLIAM G. WEBB, Brigadier-General, Twenty-second Brigade Texas State Troops to Lieutenant Col. H. L. WEBB, Assistant Adjutant-General, & c.[8]

COLONEL: On Thursday last a committee of Germans waited on me at La Grange, professing to represent 120 Germans of Fayette County, and presented a written declaration, in which they set forth the situation of their families, and stated their willingness to defend the State, provided they had guarantees that their families should be supported in their absence, but they expressly declared that they declined to take the oath to the Confederate States, because they knew of no law requiring State troops to take that oath. The declaration also stated in substance that they were called upon to defend principles far removed from them.

The Governor has the original declaration, and will send a copy to me and also to you, and I request that you wait for the receipt of the paper in order that you may judge the more fairly of its contents, as my memory may not serve me fully. The declaration, however, will support an indictment and arrest under the State laws, and it is the purpose of the Governor to have the ringleaders arrested and dealt with. The punishment is the penitentiary, not less than two nor more than five years.

The Governor arrived at La Grange on Thursday last and remained until Saturday and saw this committed, and gave them a very plain, positive talk, which I have no doubt had a good effect, and I have hope that the victory at Galveston and the knowledge of the conspirators of our being on the alert will have a good effect, and that most of the men will come to the rendezvous at this p lace to-day, it being the day fixed for it, but if there should be any reverse to our arms or a landing in force I anticipate trouble.

I have sent commissioners to all the disaffected regions–men of influence, true to our cause–who have used persuasion and mild

8 Copyright in the Public Domain.

representations of the consequences to the conspirators, and a happy effect has been the consequence; and my belief now is that a few will desert, but that a large majority of the disaffected will come here to-day. I am credibly informed that one man declared to B. B. Hudnall that he and others meant to go, but that at a good opportunity they would hoist the white flag and go over to the enemy. I am now trying to get this statement on oath, and will, if able, submit it in form.

In conclusion, I will state that this movement is not confined alone to Germans, but men of our own race and country are concerned in it. Mild measures have been determined upon by the State officers as long as they will avail, but after the men are all (that will go) got into service then the Governor intends to deal with the ringleaders.

Yours, very truly,
P. S.–At present please address me
here at Columbus.

Document 6

Alleyton, January 21, 1863, William G. Webb, Brigadier-General, Twenty-second Brigade Texas State Troops to J. C. PEMBERTON, Lieutenant-General, Commanding[9]

SIR: The Germans and others who had been in rebellion have all quaintly submitted to the draft and all have come to the different rendezvous and been enrolled as soldiers. Those who were not drafted and are at home profess to be loyal fund promise to submit cheerfully to the laws of the State and Confederacy. I shall soon hear from all the disaffected of the country, and will advise you if the favorable reports are trued.

Colonel Hardneman's command are the most disorderly, outrageous set of men I ever knew. Their officers have no control over them. They are quilt off all kinds of excesses. The planters and inhabitant generally complain to me that they nearly strip them of everything they can lay hands on, and kill their beeves and hogs and steal their

9 Copyright in the Public Domain.

poultry. I have this day issued a special order, and directed it to be read at dress parade this evening. I have talked to the officers, and they acknowledge they cannot restrain these men. I inclose a copy of the orders to show the general commanding for his approval. I also inclose a copy of an orders, which I should have sent, together with the letter asking General Magruder to issue an order to Captain Baker to remain with the Arizon Brigade.

I wish you would inclose me a few printed copies of General Orders, No. 39, issued January 8, 1863, ordering martial law in Colorado, Fayette, and Austin Counties. I have only one copy. None has reached me by letter.

After consultation with Lieutenant-Colonel Hardman and others I recommend the following-named gentlemen to be appointed provost marshals, viz: Captain William I. Hebert, for Colorado County; P. J. Shaver, esq., for Fayette County, and A. J. Bill, esq., for Austin County. You will please inform me if the commanding general will appoint the military commissioners.

HEADQUARTERS ARIZONA BRIGADE, Columbus, January 26, 1863. P. HARDEMAN, Lieutenant-Colonel, Commanding Arizona Brigade to Captain EDMUND P. TURNER, Assistant Adjutant-General.[10]

SIR: The general commanding wishes to know why I have not reported. In reply I would say that I have made two reports to headquarters, and think it very strange that they have not made their appearance.

The Germans in this section have become very quiet. Nearly all of them have gone into the militia service. I have has scouts out in the country in different directions. They report everything quiet. I start out myself this morning with a detachment of 50 men. I understand there

10 Copyright in the Public Domain.

are some of the leaders of the insurrection still in the country that have not gone into service. I will hunt them up and report to headquarters on my return. Brigadier-General Webb, of La Grange, is here; he reports everything going on monthly in that country; says there was considerable excitement there at one time.

I will report on my return from this expedition.

I have the honor to be, very respectfully, your obedient servant,

Document 8

HDQRS. DIST. OF TEXAS, NEW MEXICO, AND ARIZONA, Houston, February 11, 1863. Colonel J. BANKHEAD MAGRUDER to His Excellency F. R. LUBBOCK, Governor of the State of Texas.[11]

I am glad to be able to inform you that order and a better state of feeling are reported as existing in the disaffected regions. I have confined the declaration of martial law to the three counties of Colorado Austin, and Fayette, in which this disaffection showed itself. I hope soon to see the ordinary tribunals again in operation. The ringleaders, who have been apprehended, were by order turned over to the civil authorities, as these acts were committed prior to my declaration of martial law. Not being able to see you, as I desired, and being averse to interfering with the industrial pursuits of the country, unless demanded by necessity, I have ordered the militia recently called out at my request to return to their homes after depositing their arms with the ordnance officer at Houston. The expulsion of the enemy from our coast made it unnecessary for them to remain longer together. Their arms will be placed in the hands of volunteers, who will be stationed at convenient places for the enforcement of order and the protection of loyal citizens, wails they will be ready at any moment to repel invasion. In the mean time the militia called out has been arranged into companies and can be assembled at

11 Copyright in the Public Domain.

very short notice. Would it not a good plan to pursue the same course in other parts of the State?

I am informed that there are a great many deserters and stragglers in Texas from our armies in the field, and I respectfully recommend that the State brigadier-generals be ordered by Your Excellency to arrest all such and send them to the nearest military post or camp, whether conscript or not. I have ordered the provost-general to order his agents throughout the States to arrest such persons, whether officers or enlisted men, but think the aid of the State brigadier-generals would be of value.

I write in great haste and merely glance at these subjects, knowing whatever depends message and concur most heartily in your views, and in concluding cannot but express to you Governor, the sincere gratification it affords me to feel that I am supported so ably and so cordially by the Executive of the State which I am here to defend, and in whose welfare I feel so deep an interest.

Very respectfully,

your obedient servant,

Document 9

ALLEYTON, [TEX.], February 11, 1863. HENRY L. WEBB, Lieutenant-Colonel and Assistant Adjutant-General, to Captain EDMUND P. TURNER, Assistant Adjutant-General.[12]

SIR: I have just returned from visiting Colonel Hardeman at Columbus. He has been very sick, but is now recovering, and will be fit for duty in a few days. He desires met to inform the general commanding that there is one small company and a squad of from 15 to 20 men encamped in the village of Columbus, called Coopwood's battalion. It appears Coopwood had authority to raise a battalion, but failed to do so, and abandoned the attempt, so Colonel Hardman informs me, and Colonel Hardman also

12 Copyright in the Public Domain.

requests me to ask the commanding general to dismount the command and assign them to some command. They are now doing no service, but are insubordinate and committing depredations on the citizens of the village. Complaints were made to me, and I requested the officer in command, during the illness of Colonel Hardeman (Colonel Madison), to order them out of town to a new camping ground. This he informed me to-day he had done. I would respectfully recommend they should be dismounted and assigned to some corps where theine services may be made valuable. I sent the prisoners that we had in confinement at Columbus to the provost-marshals of the counties of Fayette and Austin, with direction for them to turn them over to the civil authorities. The escort were commanded by lieutenants belonging to Captain Rountrees' company. The one who commanded the escort to La Grange, Fayette County, has returned, and informs me that on his arrival at the county seat the prisoners were turned over to a magistrate, who immediately discharged them all and permitted them to return to their homes. I sent them to the provost-marshal under the impression that the civil authorities would confine the prisoners until the district attorney (Colonel Delaney) could collect his evidence and proof and then go into trial. The escort to Austin County has not returned. I will visit La Grange, as I known (unless I am much deceived) that evidence sufficient can be procured to convict a part of them.

Colonel Hardman has ordered Captain Rountree, with his company, into Austin County, about 30 miles from here, into the disaffected district, where there is an abundance of subsistence and forage, with orders to suppress andy insurrectionary movements among the citizens by disarming and arresting them. Captain Rountree's company is composed of good men, who are subordinate, and he is a prudent man himself, who will act with discretion, and his men will not trespass on the person on property of the people.

I have the honor to be, very respectfully, your obedient servant,

ALLEYTON, [TEX.], February 18, 1863. HENRY L. WEBB, Lieutenant-Colonel and Assistant Adjutant-General, to Captain EDMUND P. TURNER, Assistant Adjutant-General.[13]

SIR: I anticipated the commanding general's order on the petition of the women of Austin County, which I only received this day. It was left at the hotel at Columbus, at which place I received it. I visited the town of New Ulm and called on most of the persons who made the affidavits, and I find their statements to me differ materially from their statements to the general. They all say the injuries they received were indicted by two men named MacElroy, two named Henderson, and one other a straggling soldier belonging, it is believed, to General Sibley's brigade, whose name I have not learned; but Lieutenant Stone, who commanded the detachment, says be thinks he can get it and will inform me. From what I have already learned it appears Lieutenant Stone called on the MacElroys and Henderson to lead him during the night to the houses of the disaffected Germans. The men he employed were enemies of the Germans generally, and no doubt took him to the houses of innocent persons. He divided his command into two squads, went with one himself and the other a non-commissioned officer, so as to make all the arrest at about the same time, and he says he knew nothing of the outrages being committed until some time after he had removed the prisoners and the persons who committed the crimes had left him. He denies having struck a woman with the hilt of his sword. He is apparently a mild, good man, but unfit to command, not enforcing subordination and discipline. I have no doubt but the soldiers behaved baldly by pushing the women away from their husbands and some bruises were inflicted, but they all say the serious injuries were inflicted by the guides employed by Lieutenant Stone. The lieutenant says he would have arrested these men and brought them prisoners to Columbus if he had known in time that they had committed these outrages on the women and children. I told him the officer in command

13 Copyright in the Public Domain.

was answerable for the conduct of his me and for that of all persons he employs.

Colonel Hardeman intended making all the arrests himself; started out for that purpose, was taken sick, and was compelled to return without accomplishing his object, and then sent out Lieutenant Stone (as he assured me to-day), having the greatest confidence in his discretion. I will carry out the order of the general fully. I go to the counties of Austin and Fayette in the morning, and will see all the parties complaining and look into the matter closely, and have the arrests made of all I can get hold of who were concerned, and report to the general through you on Tuesday next. I assured all the citizens of the county course I saw that the commanding general would pursue the very course he has, by ordering the arrest and punishment of all persons who trespassed on the rights and privileges of the people, and that he was the last man who would suffer violence to be used forward persons arrested or to their families.

I inclose one communication from Captain Garey, quartermaster, and one from Colonel Delaney.* Please lay them before the general for his decision and action.

I have the honor to be, very respectfully, your obedient servant,

P. S. I will have the affidavits taken anew before a disinterested justice, and get a good and reliable interpreter, as none of these persons speak English. I will endeavor to have justice done all parties.

Document 11

COLUMBUS, February 23, 1863. Report of Lieutenant J. Wheeler concerning certain charges preferred against Lieutenant R. H. Stone by certain German citizens of New Ulm and its vicinity.[14]

COLUMBUS, February 23, 1863.

14 Copyright in the Public Domain.

I have visited the following-named citizens and investigated the matter of Lieutenant Stone's conduct among them as thoroughly as it lay in my power to do: Messrs.—Rouge,—Mitauk,—Honbold, Z. Darbro,—Wagner, justice of the peace.

I visited the above-named citizens and conversed with them through an interpreter relative to the maltreatment reported to have been imposed upon them by Lieutenant R. H. Stone or men under his command. They all state that they received no abuse whatever at the hands of Lieutenant Stone or any of his men, and that they all acted gentlemanly and with utmost propriety. Mrs. Rouge, the lady who is reported to have been so badly misused, state that she received no injury at the hands of Lieutenant Stone, and she does not think from any of the men under his command; that Lieutenant Stone did not come into her house, and that she was injured, but to the best of her knowledge the injury she received was at the hands of men who were not under Lieutenant Stone's command, but were citizens, neighbors, living in that vicinity, and not from any of Lieutenant Stone's command; that she was knocked down, not by any of Lieutenant Stone's command, and that she received one or two scratches from a bayonet, whether it was thrust at her or whether in the confusion of he moment, which she thinks most likely, she ran against, it, she cannot tell; that she received a wound in the forehead by being struck with the butt of a gun, but says the blow was not aimed at her; that being excited and alarmed for her husband's safety she accidentally ran against it; and that she is confident, from the general conduct and demeanor of the lieutenant and the men of his command, that they indented no injury or insult to her whatever.

The citizens above mentioned also stated that Lieutenant Stone acted in no way unbecoming an officer and a gentleman-he nor any one of his command; that they wish no injustice done him, and if the above statement of facts is not sufficient to clear him of any imputation upon his honor as an officer that they can make affidavit to abundant testimony that will.

They state, however, that there some citizens along from the neighborhood, who did not appear to be under command of any one, who acted in a very ungentlemanly manner; they recognized in those parties their immediate neighbors, and state that, if any blame whatever could attach to Lieutenant Stone, it might be that he did not exercise sufficient authority over those citizens as he did over his own men.

All of which is respectfully submitted.

WM. J. WHELLER,
Lieutenant, Company A,
First Regiment Arizona Brigade,

Section 5.
Peaceful Overtures?

By the end of 1865, the Union Army had made significant advances to secure victory in the Civil War. In November of 1864, Texas legislators gathered to draft this resolution. Note the proposed conditions and stipulations. Considering the position of Texas and the other Confederate states, were these proposed conditions realistic?

Questions

1. What were the primary concerns noted in this document?
2. Were Texans truly seeking peace with the Union?
3. What was the probable reaction of the United States Government to this resolution?

Document 1

HOUSE OF REPRESENTATIVES, January 19, 1865—Laid on the Table and Ordered to Be Printed[15]

RESOLUTIONS

Of the State of Texas, concerning peace, reconstruction, and independence. (edited by R. Minten)

WHEREAS, among the political parties of the United States the question of a re-union of those States with those of the Confederacy is being agitated, and in order to promote such re-union it is urged that

15 Copyright in the Public Domain.

delegates be chosen from each of the States in the Confederacy and in the Union, to meet in Convention to reform the Constitution of the United States, which proposition is coupled with the quasi pledge, that such amendment shall be made to the Constitution as will forever guarantee the institution of African slavery in the States in this Confederacy; and, Whereas, it is possible that the political party in the United States advocating that proposition may prevail at the approaching election in choosing the Executive of that Government, and that consequently the foregoing proposition may be attempted to be made to the States of the Confederacy; Now, we of the State of Texas, believing that it is proper to meet such proposition in advance, have resolved as follows:

Resolution 1st. Be it Resolved by the Legislature of the State of Texas, That neither the above proposition nor any other can be made to the people of this State by the United States or any other foreign people, the government of the Confederate States being the only organ of the States in the Confederacy, for the transaction of business with foreign nations, and such proposition, if made at all, must be made to the government of this States, and, if made to the government of this State, will not be entertained.

Resolution 2nd. That we recognize in that proposition no good faith, but merely an insidious policy, to "divide and conquer;" a policy through which it is hoped to detach some of the States from the Confederacy, thereby to weaken and demoralize the rest..

Resolution 3rd. That it will be well for the people of the North to understand, even at this late day, that the Southern States did not secede from the Union upon any question such as the mere preservation of the slave property of their citizens. But, that being free and sovereign States, they were resolved to preserve their freedom and their sovereignty. They were free to govern themselves as they, and not others, saw fit ... And after nearly four years of arduous war, these States are still unwavering in their resolution to preserve their freedom and their sovereignty, without which all else is valueless.

Resolution 4th. That could the present war and all its horrors be blotted out of our memories, our past experience while in the Union would warn us from any re-union with the people of the North.

Resolution 5th. But we could not if we would, banish from our memory the inhumanities of this war. Our enemies have repudiated every principle of civilized warfare. They have withdrawn their felons from Jails and Penitentiaries, have recruited from the scum of Europe, and armed our own slaves, in order to procure an army sufficiently atrocious for their purpose; and this army has been launched upon us with the declared object of our extermination. Poisoned weapons have been manufactured and used. Exchange of prisoners has been refused until the success of our armies extorted a cartel, and the terms of this have been violated by them whenever the varying fortune of the field made it apparently advantageous to do so. Our countrymen when captured have been removed to rigorous climes, and subjected to every hardship, that thus they might be destroyed. Non-combatants have been murdered. Indiscriminate onslaught has been made upon tottering age and tender youth. Our chaste and defenceless women have been submitted to outrage worse than death. Peaceful villages have been bombarded, and happy homes plundered and burnt ... Desolation has marched with their armies. Religious services have been prohibited to ministers of the gospel of peace have been incarcerated and silenced, and sacriligious hands have been laid upon our sacred alters. Lying to themselves, and pretending to the rest of the world that they are fighting the battle of freedom for four millions of happy and contented negroes, they are attempting the enslavement of eight millions of freemen. With devilish mockery of philanthropy, they have deluded and dragged these negroes from their comfortable homes to use them as screens from our weapons in the day of battle, and they have sent them by thousands to painful death by neglect, exposure and starvation. Words can not express the malignity in their hearts of the atrocity of their deeds, exceeding as they do all that was ever conceived by men from the Scythian down to the Comanche ... The people of the North have never failed, when the opportunity was presented, to render ovations to the most transcendent among the criminals, while their press has been constant in its laudation and their orators and preachers have cried out "well done." Army, government, and people, have united to make the name of Yankee, suggestive as it was before of fraud, now the synonym of barbarism and baseness.

Resolution 6th. By the just pride of the manhood and the virtue which we claim as individuals and as a people; by the divine command which warns us not to walk in the way with the wicked; by the memory of our murdered dead; by the sight of the bereaved mothers, widows, sisters, daughters and orphans in our land; by the heart brokenness of trampled virtue; and by our desolated hearths, we are forbidden to admit a thought of further association with the people of the North. Our heroic soldiers, the living, and the martyred dead, forbid it; and our trust in God forbids it.

Resolution 7th. We declare that we are earnestly desirous of peace, but we say no less distinctly that it must be coupled with our independence. And if the people of the United States be really disposed to terminate the war, they will best prove that disposition by making their proposition to the Government of the Confederate States, which alone can entertain it.

Resolution 8th. That a copy of these resolutions be transmitted to the President of the Confederate States, to each of our Senators and Representatives in Congress, and to the Governor of each State in the Confederacy.

Approved, November 12, 1864.

6 The Post-Civil War African American Experience

Section 1. Emancipation

On June 19, 1865, General Gordon Granger read the Emancipation Proclamation at Galveston, Harbor. For many African Americans, this day, now known as "Juneteenth," is the Fourth of July for African Americans. The following testimony about slave emancipation in Texas was gathered by the Federal Writers' Project (part of the WPA) as part of its interviews with ex-slaves.

Questions

1. How prepared with ex-slaves for freedom? What kinds of education or economic resources did ex-slaves possess after the Civil War?
2. What kinds of jobs were available to ex-slaves
3. What is their attitude toward their former white masters?
4. From what you read, what was the attitude of former slave masters once their slaves were freed.

Narrative 1

Felix Haywood[1], born a slave in Raleigh, North Carolina, gained his freedom in San Antonio, Texas, in the summer of 1865 when word finally reached Texas. In this interview, Haywood recalls the day of emancipation.

Soldiers, all of a sudden, was everywhere—coming in bunches, crossing and walking and riding. Everyone was a-singing. We was all walking on golden clouds. Hallelujah!

Union forever

Hurrah, boys, hurrah!

Although I may be poor;

I'll never be a slave

Shouting the battle cry of freedom.

Everybody went wild. We felt like heroes, and nobody had made us that way but ourselves. We was free. Just like that, we was free. It didn't seem to make the whites mad, either. They went right on giving us food just the same. Nobody took our homes away, but right off colored folks started on the move. They seemed to want to get closer to freedom, so they'd know what it was—like it was a place or a city. Me and my father stuck, close as a lean tick to a sick kitten. The Gudlows started us out on a ranch. My father, he'd round up cattle—unbranded cattle—for the whites. They was cattle that they belonged to, all right; they had gone to find water 'long the San Antonio River and the Guadalupe. Then the whites gave me and my father some cattle for our own. My father had his own brand—7 B)—and we had a herd to start out with of seventy.

We knowed freedom was on us, but we didn't know what was to come with it. We thought we was going to get rich like the white folks. We thought we was going to be richer than the white folks, 'cause we was stronger and knowed how to work, and the whites didn't, and they didn't have us to work

1 Felix Haywood, from *Slave Narratives: A Folk History of Slavery in the United States From Interviews*, vol. XVI. Copyright in the Public Domain.

for them any more. But it didn't turn out that way. We soon found out that freedom could make folks proud, but it didn't make 'em rich.

Did you ever stop to think that thinking don't do any good when you do it too late? Well, that's how it was with us. If every mother's son of a black had thrown 'way his hoe and took up a gun to fight for his own freedom along with the Yankees, the war'd been over before it began. But we didn't do it. We couldn't help stick to our masters. We couldn't no more shot 'em than we could fly. My father and me used to talk 'bout it. We decided we was too soft and freedom wasn't going to be much to our good even if we had a education.

After the War, Master Colonel Sims went to git the mail and so he call Daniel Ivory, the overseer, and say to him, "Go round to all the quarters and tell all the niggers to come up, I got a paper to read to 'em. They're free now, so you kin git you another job, 'cause I ain't got no more niggers which is my own." Niggers come up from the cabins nappy-headed, jest lak they gwine to the field. Master Colonel Sims say, "Caroline (that's my mammy), you is free as me. Pa said bring you back and I'se gwina do jest that. So you go on and work and I'll pay you and your three oldest chillun \$10.00 a month a head and\$4.00 fer Harriet," that's me, and then he turned to the rest and say "Now all you'uns will receive \$10.00 a head till the crops is laid by." Don't you know before he got half way thoo', over half them niggers wasgone.

***Harriet Robinson*[2]**, enslaved in Texas, interviewed in Oklahoma, 1937.

After the War, Master Colonel Sims went to git the mail and so he call Daniel Ivory, the overseer, and say to him, "Go round to all the quarters and tell all the niggers to come up, I got a paper to read to'em. They're free now, so you kin git you another job, 'cause I ain't got no more niggers which is my own." Niggers come up from the cabins nappy-headed, jest lak they gwine to the field. Master Colonel Sims say, "Caroline (that's

2 Harriet Robinson, from *Slave Narratives: A Folk History of Slavery in the United States From Interviews*, vol. XIII. Copyright in the Public Domain.

my mammy), you is free as me. Pa said bring you back and I'se gwina do jest that. So you go on and work and I'll pay you and your three oldest chillun $10.00 a month a head and $4.00 fer Harriet," that's me, and then he turned to the rest and say "Now all you'uns will receive $10.00 a head till the crops is laid by." Don't you know before he got half way thoo', over half them niggers was gone.

Narrative 3

Tom Holland[3], enslaved in Texas, interviewed in Texas, c. 1937.

I 'lieve they ought to have gived us somethin' when we was freed, but they turned us out to graze or starve. Most of the white people turned the Negroes slam loose. We stayed a year with missis and National Humanities Center 6 then she married and her husband had his own workers and told us to git out. We worked for twenty and thirty cents a day then, and I fin'ly got a place with Dr. L. J. Conroe. But after the war the Negro had a hard struggle, 'cause he was turned loose jus' like he came into the world and no education or 'sperience.

Narrative 4

Martin Jackson[4], enslaved in Texas, interviewed in Texas, 1937.

The master's name was usually adopted by a slave after he was set free. This was done more because it was the logical thing to do and the easiest way to be identified than it was through affection for the master. Also, the government seemed to be in a almighty hurry to have us get names. We had to register as someone, so we could be citizens. Well, I got to thinking about all us slaves that was going to take the name Fitzpatrick. I made up my mind I'd find me a different one. One of my grandfathers in Africa was called Jeaceo, and so I decided to be Jackson.

3 Tom Holland, from *Slave Narratives: A Folk History of Slavery in the United States From Interviews*, vol. XVI. Copyright in the Public Domain.

4 Martin Jackson, from *Slave Narratives: A Folk History of Slavery in the United States From Interviews*, vol. XVI,. Copyright in the Public Domain.

Section 2. Reading Between the Lines: Post-War Violence Against Freed Slaves

After Emancipation, the relationship between slaves and masters changed dramatically. Both had to navigate new social and economic territory with little guidance. The following records from the Bureau Of Refugees are the official transcripts from the Trial of John Echols, who was accused of killing his former slave, Kit. As you read through the testimonies, try to determine the motivations of the trial participants. Make a list of the facts and recreate the events that led to the fatal confrontation.

Questions

1. Who conducted the trial?
2. What part did John Echols play in the trial proceedings?
3. Do you consider the trial proceedings and outcome to be fair? Explain your answer.

Document 1

Testimony in trial of John Echols,[5] Phoebe Jones (Freedwoman) Testimony in relation to the killing of her son Kit by his former Master John Echols

Records of the Assistant Commissioner for the State of Texas
Bureau of Refugees, Freedmen and Abandoned Lands, 1865–1869
National Archives Microfilm Publication M821 Roll 32
"Miscellaneous Records Relating to Murders and Other Criminal Offenses Committed in Texas 1865–1868"

Brazos Bottom
Burleson Co., Tex.
Dec. 18th, 1865
Phoebe Jones (Freedwoman)

5 Copyright in the Public Domain.

Testimony in relation to the killing of her son Kit by his former Master John Echols
Phoebe (Freedwoman) being duly sworn testifies as follows—

On the day that my son was killed by our former Master Mr. John Echols I was laying in my bed sick when my son (Kit) came from the gin house & asked me what was the matter. I told him I did not know what was the matter. He said that he would go to the house and see the old man (Mr. Echols) & see what he had beaten Harriet about (Harriet is my son's wife). I told him he had better not go. He did go however, & in a few moments I heard the gun & I jumped out of bed & ran out in the yard to my son whom I found lying on the ground dead. He only breathed twice after I reached him. This is all I know about it.
Cross examination by the Agt. F. Bureau

Q. Did your son appear excited when he came into the house as you stated.
A. No.
Q. Did he take a knife when he started to see "The Old Man."
A. Yes he had a knife in his headband.
Q. Have you got the knife in your possession.
A. Yes I have.
Q. When you saw your son after he was shot was the knife in his hands or near him.
A. Yes, the knife was out of the headband & lying on the ground underneath him.
Q. Had you heard previous to this transaction of any threats made by your son against Mr. Echols.
A. No.
Q. How long did you belong to Mr. Echols before you were free.
A. About 15 years.
Q. During that time has he treated you & all of his slaves kindly & taken good care of them.
A. Yes.
Q. Since you were made free have you discovered that he treated you or them differently.
A. No.
Q. When was your son buried.

A. On the evening of Monday following the day he was shot.

Q. Do you know anything of Mr. Echols settling accounts with the freedmen whom he employed.

A. I saw the money they received which was specie.

Q. Did you ever hear anything about Mr. Echols saying he did not want your son to stay on the plantation any longer.

A. Yes I heard my son say so—& Mr. Echols offered them wagons to move.

Cross examination by the accused.
The witness testified as follows.

Q. Did I not take two white gentlemen with me to your quarters & tell you in their presence that I wanted you & others who were not going to stay on the place to leave it peaceably & without any further trouble.

A. Yes sir.

Q. Do you know anything about the clubs which was picked up near the house.

A. Yes. The boys were in the habit of carrying them at night for a year or more. They did not carry them in the day time. The one shown me now belonged to my son Kit—who was killed.

Q. When I entered your house on Saturday morning & had to make Harriet get out of bed and leave the house did you see me beat her.

A. No—I heard & saw you trying to make Harriet (my son's wife) get out of bed but did not see you beat her.

Q. Do you know to whom the larger club (marked A. I.) belonged—or who had it in possession at the time your son was killed.

A. I do not.

I certify & acknowledge that the foregoing statement & answers are correct & I have made them under oath.
Phoebe (X) Jones
Witnesses
John Goodwin
W. F. Grant

Document 2

Harriet Echols, Freedwoman Testimony in relation to the killing of her husband Kit by his former Master John Echols[6]

Records of the Assistant Commissioner for the State of Texas
Bureau of Refugees, Freedmen and Abandoned Lands, 1865–1869
National Archives Microfilm Publication M821 Roll 32
"Miscellaneous Records Relating to Murders and Other Criminal Offenses Committed in Texas 1865–1868"

Brazos Bottom
Burleson Co., Tex.
Dec. 18th 1868
Harriet Echols, Freedwoman

Testimony in relation to the killing of her husband Kit by his former Master John Echols

Harriet Echols (Freedwoman) being duly sworn testifies as follows—

On Saturday morning before daylight (Dec. 8th) Mr. Echols came to Phoebe's (my mother-in-law) house where I was in bed & commenced to beat me. My husband was at the gin house baling cotton. The old man (Mr. Echols) went to the corn crib & started to the house with a sack of corn. My husband Kit followed behind him which I saw from the corner of Phoebe's house. This is all I know about it until I saw the old man shoot my husband.

Harriet (X) Echols
Witnesses

Robt. (X) Graham Co. "B" 37th Ill. Vol. Reg.
W. T. Grant
Examined by the Agt. of the Freedmen's Bureau the witness testifies as follows—

6 Copyright in the Public Domain.

Q. How long before daylight on Saturday morning did Mr. Echols come to Phoebe's house.
A. About half an hour.

Q. How long had your husband been then gone to the press.
A. I do not know.
Q. Do you know that your husband had gone to the press.
A. No I do not—I only heard so.
Q. When your husband followed behind Mr. Echols—from the corn crib towards the house—do you know whether he had any weapon.
A. Yes he had a knife.
Q. Did you see the knife after he was killed & if so where.
A. When I got to him after he fell the knife was lying under him.
Q. Was it out of the headband.
A. Yes.
Q. In what part of the body was your husband shot.
A. In the right shoulder.
Q. Had you previous to your husband being killed heard him or any other of the servants on the place make any threats against Mr. Echols or any of his family.
A. No sir.
Q. Did not Mr. Echols frequently tell you & your husband after you were made free that he did not want you to stay on his plantation. That he wanted you both to leave & would not pay you for staying any longer. And did he pay you or not.
A. Yes he often told us to go away & offered to furnish wagons to move us. And he also paid us for all the labor we performed for him.
Q. State what your mother said about the wages Mr. Echols paid you.
A. I don't know anything about that.
Q. How long did you belong to Mr. Echols before you were free.
A. He raised me from a child.
Q. During the time you were his slave was he in the habit of treating you & his other slaves kindly, supplying your wants in food, clothing, nursing &c.
A. Yes he was.
Q. Since you were made free has he treated you or them differently.
A. He has not.
Q. Was he ever in the habit of whipping you or others.

A. Not much.
I certify that the foregoing answers were given under oath & are correct.

Harriet (X) Echols
Witness
H. Cooper
W. F. Grant
Freedwoman Phebe Jones recalled

Q by the agent of the Freedmen's Bureau. At what time in the morning did you hear did you hear in the morning Mr. Echols in the house. (transcribed exactly as written)
A. About sunrise.
2nd Q. Is the knife now in my possession the knife Kit carried the morning that he was killed.
A. It is.

Phebe (X) Jones
Test.

Thos. L. Goodwin
J. C. Goodwin

Document 3

John Echols Voluntary Statement of Facts in relation to his killing a freedman named "Kit"[7]

Records of the Assistant Commissioner for the State of Texas
Bureau of Refugees, Freedmen and Abandoned Lands, 1865–1869
National Archives Microfilm Publication M821 Roll 32
"Miscellaneous Records Relating to Murders and Other Criminal Offenses Committed in Texas 1865–1868"

Brazos Bottom

7 Copyright in the Public Domain.

Burleson Co., Tex.
Dec. 18th, 1865
John Echols
Voluntary statement of facts in relation to his killing a freedman named "Kit"

State of Texas
Burleson County

John Echols having been arrested for shooting a certain Freedman named Christopher Jones alias "Kit"—& being duly examined made the following statement of facts—viz—

I was born in the state of Virginia, raised in Ala. & emigrated to Texas in 1835 where I have resided & followed the occupation of a planter ever since. For the last 28 or 29 years I have been a citizen of this (Burleson County).

I am now sixty three years of age & consequently was unable to take any part in the war. But on its termination I acquainted my slaves with the change in their status & read to them all military orders which concerned them.

I also entered into a verbal contract with them & agreed to pay them $10.00 per month for their services while saving my growing crops. I complied with this contract allowing them wages from about the 1st of January last & paid them in silver & gold about the 27th of November 1865. After this settlement with which they declared themselves satisfied I told three of the men viz, Christopher alias "Kit," Black Jim & Washington that I would not have them on the place if they would pay me $100.00 apiece. That I desired them to leave my premises in peace & offered them the use of my wagons to move their effects & I told them they were free to go & I would not interfere or molest them.

They would not go, but remained on the place, occupying my houses & I received messages & heard from the other negroes that the negroes I have named declared they would die before they would go.

On or about the 8th day of Dec. 1865 (Saturday) about an hour after sunrise the boy Kit came to the house I occupied when visiting the plantation when I was alone, engaged in shelling corn (as none of the negroes would do it, or any other work although I offered to pay them). Upon seeing him at the door I asked him what he wanted. He replied that he had understood from a negro named Jeff that I had told Major Dudley (a neighbor) that he had better not hire him (Kit), that he was a bad boy & I did not want him to be hired in the neighborhood. I then got up & walked nearly to the door without any weapon & with no intention of any violence but simply intending to talk to the negro & induce him to go away as I desired.

He immediately drew a large butcher knife about 10 inches long and commenced advancing upon me with the knife drawn & in a manner which induced me to apprehend that he intended to attack me.

I instantly retreated to the back side of the house & seized a double barreled shot gun which was standing in the corner & returned with it towards the door. I leveled the gun upon him & told him I would kill him if he did not go off & let me alone but that I did not wish to do so & wanted him to go off.

When I leveled the gun he commenced to back off but without turning from me. I then took the gun down & he instantly commenced advancing upon me a second time with his knife still in his hand. I also saw two other negro men running up on the other side of the house—seeing the negro Kit again advancing & believing that the other negroes were about to join him in his attack, I raised my gun a second time & fired upon him. He ran about 20 paces & fell dead.

Instantly I turned towards a crowd of negroes who had collected & saw a brother of the boy I had shot named Bob making violent efforts to get loose from negroes who were holding & restraining him from attacking me. Seeing this I told them to let him loose as I was prepared for him too. But a negro named Sam & others took him off & carried him to the woods, since which time I have not seen him.

I thus resumed my occupation of shelling corn & remained in or near the house until my son arrived on the place.

It is proper for me to state also that some of the negroes ran off when I shot Kit & we found upon the ground they had occupied a large club evidently intended & proposed for a weapon of distinction. A few days afterward a still larger one was found & produced.

I told the negroes to go to Millican & report the facts to the authorities. And seeing the negro remained unburied I told them they ought to attend to it.

I then remained at home pursuing my usual avocations until I was arrested by a detachment of soldiers sent from Millican for the purpose who arrived about Tuesday about noon on Tuesday 11th inst.

When I saw them coming I told them to stop & come in as I presumed I was the person they were looking for.

Nothing but my delicate health & the extremely cold & inclement weather prevented me from reporting the facts in person to the military authorities. And I resigned doing so as soon as the storm abated.

In conclusion I would state that I owned about 70 slaves who were liberated last summer and that the boys Kit, Black Jim & Washington were the only ones who had occasioned me any serious difficulty before or since.

These boys however have been very troublesome & made threats about my son in the event of his continuing to manage the place, which induced me to take my son away & assume personal superintendence of my affairs in order to avoid any collision.

Upon investigation too, I think it will be found that I was a kind & indulgent Master & that some of my negroes were turbulent, dangerous & violent, facts which can be established by the evidence of both whites & blacks in my vicinity.

Witness my hand this 18th day of December 1865.

John Echols

Document 4

Daniel Tasker (Freedman) Testimony in relation to the killing of a freedman named Kit by his former Master John Echols[8]

Records of the Assistant Commissioner for the State of Texas
Bureau of Refugees, Freedmen and Abandoned Lands, 1865–1869
National Archives Microfilm Publication M821 Roll 32
"Miscellaneous Records Relating to Murders and Other Criminal Offenses Committed in Texas 1865–1868"

8 Copyright in the Public Domain.

Brazos Bottom
Burleson Co., Tex.
Dec. 18th 1865
Daniel Tasker (Freedman)
Testimony in relation to the killing of a freedman named Kit by his former Master John Echols
Daniel Tasker (Freedman) being duly sworn testifies as follows—

On the morning that Kit was killed I was in the corn crib shucking corn & knew nothing about the matter until I heard the report of the gun. When I ran out to see what was the matter, I could only see a crowd of the negros standing in the yard hollering & screaming but did not see Kit until late in the evening. I went to where his body was lying. That is all I know about it.

Daniel (X) Tasker
Witness
W. F. Grant
Charles Himes Co. "R" 37th Ill. In.

Being examined by the Agent of the Freedmen's Bureau the witness testified as follows—

Q. How old are you.
A. Seventy eight.
Q. How long have you lived with Mr. Echols.
A. About thirty three years.
Q. Were you at all related to the boy Kit.
A. Not at all.
Q. Had you at any time previous to Kit's death heard either him or others make any threats against Mr. Echols or any of his family.
A. I have not sir.
Q. Were you in the corn crib when Mr. Echols went to the corn crib for a bag of corn & if so at what time in the day was it?
A. I was & it was near 8 o'clock in the morning.

Q. You say that you have belonged to & lived with Mr. Echols over thirty years—during that time has he been a good & kind master to you & his other slaves?

A. He has been a kind master & both he & his wife took good care of us when we were sick. He made no difference between us—except in the case of the old negros who were more indulged.

Q. Since you were made free has he treated you or them differently.

A. No sir he has not. He has treated us with equal kindness.

Q. Did Mr. Echols read to you & explain all the orders relating to your being made free.

A. He did.

Q. After informing you all of your freedom did he make any contracts to pay you & if so did he comply with such contract.

A. He agreed to pay them for saving his crops & after the work was done he notified them to come for their money. He paid all off in gold & silver who came to him for their money.

Q. Were they satisfied with the settlement.

A. I have heard no complaint about it from any of them.

Q. When was Kit killed by Mr. Echols.

A. At Mr. Echols Plantation in Brazos Bottom, Burleson Co., Texas, on Saturday about the 8th day of Dec. 1865 about 8 o'clock in the morning.

Q. What was Kit's character.

A. He and others were in the habit of running away & staying off 5 or 6 months at a time without any good cause, running away from his work.

Q. Did you ever know Mr. Echols to whip or abuse Kit.

A. No sir I never did.

Q. When the slaves were declared free did any of them who had belonged to Mr. Echols go off. If so did he endeavor to get them back—or use any means to make them stay?

A. A good many of them left at first but all came back. Mr. Echols did not try to make them do it. He told them if they would stay & gather the crop they could all go & ?he would let them use his wagons to move away.

I certify that I have made the foregoing statement & answers under oath & that they are true.

Daniel (X) Tasker
Witness
Charles Hime Co. "R" 37th Ill. In.
H. Cooper

Document 5

Freedmen's Bureau Records—Recommendation of Mr. Echols[9]

Records of the Assistant Commissioner for the State of Texas
Bureau of Refugees, Freedmen and Abandoned Lands, 1865–1869
National Archives Microfilm Publication M821 Roll 32
"Miscellaneous Records Relating to Murders and Other Criminal Offenses Committed in Texas 1865–1868"

Recommendation of Mr. Echols

We the undersigned citizens and neighbors of John Echols respectfully represent to the Freedman's Bureau that we take pleasure in testifying that we have so far as come to our knowledge always found him a good neighbor and a kind and human master. If he had a fault in the management of his negroes it was an over indulgent leniency both during the existence of the institute of slavery and afterward.

Burleson Co., Dec. 17th 1865
John Goodwin
Thos. L. Goodwin
W. A. Green
T. W. Dudley
STATE OF TEXAS,

Department of State.

9 Copyright in the Public Domain.

I, Robert J. Townes, Secretary of State of the State of Texas, do hereby certify that the foregoing is a true and correct copy of the original, now on file in my Department. In testimony whereof, I have hereunto signed my name and caused the Seal of my Department to be affixed, at Austin, this 15th day of November, A. D., 1864.

R. J. Townes.

Section 3. Ku Klux Klan Activity in Post-War Texas

During Reconstruction, the Ku Klux Klan developed numerous branches across the former Confederate states. Its purpose was to intimidate newly-freed slaves, and Republican voters and office holders. It often resorted to violent tactics to achieve this purpose. The following letters from Donald Campbell to Texas Governor Elisha Pease and from John B. Mullen to Texas Legislator M. L. Armstrong recount Klan activity in Jefferson County and Hopkins County, Texas. Campbell referred to the K.R.S, which was the Knights of the Rising Sun, a local division of the KKK.

Questions

1. What complaints did K.R.S. members raise?
2. What was the environment like for the freedmen in Jefferson County?
3. What was Campbell's position on the situation? What solution does he propose?
4. What challenges did officials face in combatting the activities of Klan organizations?
5. What was the tone of Mullen's letter to M. L. Armstrong?
6. What forms of intimidation did Mullen experience and witness?
7. Why did the citizens of Hopkins County feel defenseless? What were their options in obtaining justice?
8. Compare the letters and discuss the similarities in details, terror strategies, and challenges to authority.

Document 1

Donald Campbell to Pease, August 25, 1868, Records of Elisha Marshall Pease, Texas Office of the Governor, Archives and Information Services Division, Texas State Library and Archives Commission[10]

Jefferson, Tuesday August 25
Hon. E.M. Pease
Austin
My Dear Sir—

The excitiment was much higher with us last night than it has ever been before. It camevery near resulting in a general riot and massacre.The K.R.S. had a meeting about 5 o'clock in the town Hall and invited Lieut Smith to be present. They had great complaints to make in regard to the negroes being armed,but not a word to say in regard to the outrages recurring here every day and night by their war party. The negroes feel that they have been outraged and that unless they protect themselves they will be killed up by these outlaws.

Threats have been made that their Church is to be burnt or torn down and they have simply armed themselves and when night comes, they go to their Church and await any attack that may be made upon it. They interfere with no one and will interfere with no one, but have determined if their Church is attacked, to die in defending it. Last night a party of Ku Kluxes went out to attack them, but through the efforts of Lieut Smith and several others, it was prevented. During the night however, the wildest excitement prevailed all over our city—horsemen from the direction of the Church were running at full speed. The Hall bell was run or six times, horns were blown in different parts of town. Yelling and shooting and all manner of things were done to alarm loyal men and freedmen. It was feared at the time that the troops would be attacked and they stood with their guns in their hands ready to resist them. But fortunately everything passed off without injury to any one. It is understood here that 300 of the expected troops have reached Marshall. If so, we may expect them here very soon. But when they come,will it be sufficient if the rebels will be quiet until they are withdrawn?

10 Copyright in the Public Domain.

This has been the practice heretofore, and the moment the troops are taken away they commence their devilment again. They must be hunted up and punished. They must be made to fear a violation and resistance of the authority of the U. States. Without it, all will go for nothing. Turning outlaws and assassins over to the Civil Authorities amounts to their sure release. They must be tried by Military Commissioners the moment they are caught and dealt with as they deserve.

Truly yours
D. Campbell

Document 2

Reign of Terror in Hopkins County[11]

Freedmen's Bureau Records–Letter from Hopkins County, Sulphur Springs, July 17, 1868

Hon. M. L. Armstrong:

Dear Sir—I am this morning situated like a mariner whose vessel is sinking, and he is dripping out slips of paper, hoping they may fall into some friendly hands, that the world may know what became of him.

The reign of terror is set up in this county. I will not undertake to give a minute description of it; time and space is not sufficient. Suffice it to say that the history of the darkest ages of the world does not, in my estimation, afford a parallel.

It commenced about the 1st of June, by brutally murdering Charles Grimes, the old freedman who was on the Board of Registrars. This occurred on Sunday night, as well as I recollect, about the 17th of June. There was not the least semblance of any provocation for the outrage. Next, I ascertained beyond a doubt that the same parties were seeking an opportunity to kill me. I was cultivating my farm two and a half miles from town. I employed hands who agreed to assist me until I could wind up my farming. Just as I was nearly through, I was waylaid by the assassins as I was returning from my farm house, but happening to see them in time I made my escape and got home. They then followed me to

11 Copyright in the Public Domain.

town the next day, and I was forced to take shelter in my house. There I remained for five days and nights, not venturing to poke my head out of doors day or night. Just at this time I ascertained that there were five wagon loads of government supplies landed here for soldiers, and at the same time one Ben Bickerstaff arrived with three men. The next day (which was day before yesterday) he attacked and took possession of all the stores, carrying off one wagon and team. He burned some of the provisions, it is said. Yesterday there was a party engaged in hauling off the goods. They were armed, and would not let any one come near enough to ascertain who they were; but the wagon tracks show where they went.

P. A. Turk, the Wagon Master, told me there were twenty or more armed men when he was robbed, all young men, mostly armed with double barreled guns and six shooters.

Mark you, Bickerstaff only had three men besides himself the day before. So you see he must have recruited 16 or 18 men here. Straws show which way the wind blows. At this juncture I was notified by those who professed to know, that I had but a few minutes to make my escape in. I saw two of the citizens, and they promised they would use their influence to save my family from being murdered; and this shows where I took up quarters.

I suppose you think strange of the murder of women and children. Ah, sir, it has already happened. About one week ago Minerva James was taken out of the house of Mr. Herman Spencer, four miles from this place, by five armed men, carried about one mile, and brutally murdered. It if had space to give you the particulars, you would say it was the most horrid murder you ever heard of.

Three days ago there was a man by the name of Flowers, taken out of his house at night and killed. The next day a party of men were carrying him to the burying ground, when they were fired into, and one man and a little boy killed, and another man dangerously wounded, receiving a shot through the lungs.

Mark you, these are all Union men. No doctor will attend the wounded man; his name is Jesse Starr, whose brother was wounded by the Shelby men; and it was his little son that was killed.

It is impossible to give the number of negroes that have been killed. There is a great many missing that have not been heard from. Four nights ago there was a freedman taken out of Buck Thomas' kitchen and carried out on the prairie and killed. There is no cause assigned or conjectured for his murder, as he was one of the most innocent of negroes. I mention this, as there is generally some pretext got up by the rebels for every murder. The would-be social class of rebels stand ever ready to fabricate false hoods and make excuses for all murders committed by their friends. The only excuse they could get up for the murder of Minerva James, was that she should have told some one (but nobody knows who) that she knew who killed Charley Grimes, and that when the soldiers came she was going to tell it. So you can see from what I have written, how things stand in this county.

I was informed by Musgrove that we would have soldiers here. They were to have been here two weeks ago; still they have not come yet, and we can hear nothing from them. I have tried to rally the Union men, but all in vain; four is all that I can get together.

The freed people have had all their arms taken away from them, and they are in the most deplorable condition of any people on earth. All that were living in the county by themselves, have been robbed of every thing of the least value-even taking the under dressing of freed women, their bed clothes; in a word every thing of the smallest value, and then driven from their homes into the woods. It is the most sickening sight I ever witnessed to see their fine corn crops now being destroyed by the stock. But I must close this sickening subject.

I am aiming to send this letter to Dallas, to have it mailed. It is impossible to have anything of the kind sent from this county by mail. The postmasters are all Ku Klux.

I see from the papers, you are doing all you can in the Convention to give protection; but if it comes at all, (which I very much doubt) it will be too late for most of the prominent Republicans. I know that I can't survive but a few days, unless there is a speedy change in our favor. They are recruiting daily. Every day makes them more bold and defiant. Every outrage they commit seems to increase their desire for something worse.

I cannot leave my family to be murdered by them. I am bound to stay near them, so that I can give them protection at night.

Show this to any one you see proper, I care not who. I don't suppose I will be alive when this comes to hand; at least the chances look slim. I prefer a martyr's grave to living a slave. I shall die the same.

Joe Easley., John B. Mullens, Henry Gregg
W. H. Jenkins, J. T. Grant, D. R. Meyers
A. Frautwein

Section 4. Offenses Against the Loyal League

In Texas and across the other former Confederate states, the Loyal League was a secret organization formed by the Republican Party during Reconstruction. Its purpose was to provide support for newly enfranchised black voters in the state. When the League achieved limited success in mobilizing the freedmen, enraged white southerners fought back. They viewed African American enfranchisement as an assault on traditional southern values and used a number of effective and appalling tactics to torment African American voters and those who assisted them.

Questions

1. Discuss several reasons why white southerners would fear and dislike the idea of black voting rights.
2. What recourse did the freedmen have to secure their rights? Describe the challenges they faced.
3. Describe the challenges that white League workers faced in trying to secure the rights and safety of freedmen.

Freedmen's Bureau Records Relating to Murders and Other Criminal Offenses Committed in Texas, Records of the Assistant Commissioner for the State of Texas, Bureau of Refugees, Freedmen and Abandoned Lands, 1865–1869[12]

The State of Texas
City of Austin

Mark Walker, colored, being duly sworn testifies as follows:—

I used to belong to William Hines. I have been living ten years in Freestone County. This year (1868) I rented ground and a cabin on the place of Dr. Gibbs in said county, in the same yard with James Eaton Haynes (colored). About the last of April I think, about seven or eight men (white) came to my house, and called "Mark, Mark, come out"—stating that they had a Captain in their company and were ordered take me to Fairfield by the Bureau from Waco. They said "We understand that you have two revolvers," and they ordered me to take them (revolvers) with me, and get ready as quick as possible. About this time, or a little before, I heard the voice of Eaton Haynes crying "Help, Help." I was asleep when they first came, and the first thing I heard was the call "Mark come out." My wife called me the same time. I did not recognize any of them 'til Cap. Davy stepped upon my gallery and said "Mr. Sheriff is this what I ordered you to do, God damn you?" He then broke down the door and came in and said Mark you know me don't you? I said "Yes Captain I do." He said that he was ordered by the Bureau at Waco to take me to Fairfield. Says I, "Cap. Davy will you let me make up a light to get my clothes," he replied, "No." I said "I am naked and I cannot go without my clothes." My wife then said "Please let my old man get his clothes." He said to her, "Shut up your G—d d—m mouth." He then said "Mark I want you take them two revolvers I understand you have, and if you want to go to shooting we are all ready for you." My wife then got my five shooter and handed it to me. Then he gathered me in the bosom and said "Come out of here I'll wait on you no longer." By this time quite a number of men were in the house, I recognized

12 Copyright in the Public Domain.

three of them, Cap. Davy, Jim Oliver and Jno. Dunn, they dragged me out of the door, threatening to shoot out my brains if I resisted. I said I would not resist, that I did not know what I had done for which they should carry me to Fairfield, they then said , "O no, I reckon not."

They carried me out over the fence and made go along with them, on the road in a trot, and one of them jerked my five shooter out of my hand. They kept saying "let us shoot him." Cap. Davy said "men obey orders, don't shoot till I give the word." They then asked me if I prayed. I told them I did. They asked me if I ever preached. I said no. They asked me if I ever fished with man's bait. I said I had not. Cap. Davy said "You went fishing Saturday didn't you?" I said I had. This was on Monday night. They then said "You caught a right smart string." I said I did. They said "You can go a fishing again tomorrow" and "you can fish with your own bait." By this time we were passing by their horses where they were hitched in a wood pasture. I said "there are some horses," they told me to shut up my mouth and come on. They took me about 3 hundred yards off the road into a bottom and made me sit down on the ground—and Cap. Davy having sat down too by me on left side, put his pistol to my left ear and jabbed it to my temples and asked me how I would like that and then said "You can report to your friend Culver tomorrow about us. He is in hell and we going to send you there too G—d d—m him." He cocked his pistol and started to put it to my temple again. I said "Mr. Davy don't shoot me, don't shoot me for God's sake," I threw up my hand and knocked the pistol off. I then jumped and run, got off about 5 feet and the pistol fired hitting me in the left leg. I fell. They said "he is down." I then got up and continued to run. They firing at me. They tried to surround and head me off but I managed to get away from them. They shot at me about a dozen times. I returned to my own house and called to my wife—she was not there. I hunted her up—she was among the colored men trying to get them to hunt me up. I then got my gun and went to Dr. Gibbs and showed him my wounds and told how it was done. He said to me that he had heard men talking about killing me for reporting to Capt. Culver about the burning the colored school house. He further said that the white people were all mad with the colored people for letting the Yankees fool them and for joining the Leagues, and as the troops were gone they would now have satisfaction.

I then left and came to Waco & from there to Austin, and went back to my home with some soldiers, and leaving my crops and many of my things came back to Austin with the soldiers. On our way back the prisoners were delivered up to some armed men. I cannot stay at home. They would kill me there.

I had no quarrell with any of these men who assaulted me. They told me that it was because I reported the burning of the school house (colored) to Capt. Culver and because I was head of the League.

During the night when I was in their hands, they told me that they intended to kill Col. Lippard and Ed Dillard and Fred Miller because they were all League men.

(signed) Mark (X) Walker
Sworn to and subscribed before me this the 18th day of June 1868.
(signed) Thad. McRae
Clerk Court on Lawlessness
A True Copy

7 The Post-Civil War Indian Wars

Prior to the Civil War, the United States had set up a series of forts across the western frontier in order to protect settlers from Indian attack. Many had been established in western Texas and along the northern border between Texas and Indian Territory in Oklahoma. During the Civil War, of course, federal troops had been withdrawn and Texans had the double duty of manning the forts and sending men to fight in the Civil War. Because the forts had been understaffed between 1861 and 1864, Plains Indians had made substantial progress in raiding Anglo settlements and reclaiming lost land in Texas. After the war ended, Indians continued to push their temporary advantage to the dismay of Texas settlers. Many of these confrontations took place along the border of Texas and Oklahoma. In a powerful 1866 letter, W. H. Whaley, a citizen of Gainesville in Cooke County, Texas, pleads with Texas Governor James W. Throckmorton to request federal assistance in dealing with the constant and devastating Indian raids. Given the chaotic environment of the Reconstruction Era, protecting the border of a former Confederate state might not have been the federal government's top priority. Nevertheless, it would have been advantageous to discourage Indian attacks in the frontier in order to encourage western settlement and development.

As you read the following letter, consider the issues surrounding this situation.

Questions

1. Whaley mentioned that the Anglo settlers had been in the area for 25 years; did they have more right to the area than the Comanche?
2. The strain and urgency were apparent in Whaley's letter. What examples of violence did he relate in the letter? Did his concerns seem genuine? Explain your answer.
3. Throckmorton's highest priority as governor was to protect the people of his state. Given his position as the governor of a former Confederate state, in what ways could he have convinced the federal government to come to the side of the people of Cooke County? What other options might he try?

Document 1

W. H. Whaley to James W. Throckmorton, September 29, 1866. Texas Indian Papers, Volume 4, #81, Archives and Information Services Division, Texas State Library and Archives Commission.[1]

Gainesville Cooke Country Texas
September 29th 1866
Gen. James W. Throckmorton
Gov of the State of Texas

Dear Sir

It is with feelings of the deepest anxiety that I address you on the present importent chrisis, the most importent that ever our county has undergone since its organiseation. We feel truly that we are in the most chritical situation that we have ever been since Cook County was organised: of late we have been raded upon by large bands of Indians and White men togather whose depradations have been of the most horrid character and they still threaten us almost daily, in so much, that nearly all the people have left the upper part of the country and Gainesville

1 Copyright in the Public Domain.

might now be called an extreme out post, On last monday the Indians and white men raders came in 6 or 7 miles of our town killed and scalped two men and carried off some 5 or 6 hundred head of horses, besides doing much other mischief, such as cutting down wagons killed work cattle and stock of every kind and runing men for their lives all over the prairie, the portion of country lying on Clare Creek and Mountain Creek has hardly been cleare of the them for the last 10 or 15 days; no one knows what the frontier people have suffered this season but those who have lived on it. and no one can feel for them and cypathise [sympathize] with there properly but those who have a just knowledge of their sufferings. Of late they come in such large bands that having no organised force, it is imposable to gather up enough citizens to handle them till they have done their mischief and gone Yo [you] have no idea Gen. of the offul state of excitement now exesting in our county, nearly every settlement west and N west of us is broken up, and the citizens who have not gone entirely off are now in-camp round our town, not knowing what to do our county is almost ruined It will not recover from this shock. I greatly fear in years, and what a pity that such a county as Cook should be so necesitated to retrigrade instead of advance in civailization and improvement. The very oldest of frontier setlers men who have stood the shock of Indian exskirsions for 25 years now have left their extreem frontier homes and are now incamped a round our town, not being able to withstand the tromendeous rades that are now being made against us, The raders are as well armed as we are, each man bareing from one to two sixshooters besids guns and they fight eaqual to any whites troops Of late our scouts have had several engagements with them, the raiders invariably getting the best of it. They generally outnumber our men 2 or 3 to one, and they cannot handle them that way for it takes man to man, Amongue these last raiders white men were seen distincly a monkst them as they pursued horses, and they were herd to speak plain English. We learned here yesterday that the fronteer bill had passed, after much debate and delay over it, in the Senate, we are informed that senator Bumpuss from Collin County done his utmost againts it, this would be some-what excuseable in a senator from the deepest interior of the state, but for a man from a cister county to our own and almost a frontier itself he is in no wise excusable I almost deem him an enemy to the white race. It is no time now to estimate indebted-ness that might accrue, when the safety of our homes and our property are at stake, our livs dael in jeopordy our women and our childrin being carried off into captivity worse than death We know Gen. that you are doing and have been doing all you can for us, but before you can give us relief If we lay still our county will be depopilated, we are trying now to organise companies for our protection till the state can come to our relief, do hasten it Gen. Before we are entirely ruined. It is generally believed that Gainsville will be the next point of attack, and you are aware how hard it is to organise troops without state or national authority. Influential and welthy citizens express backwardness in this matter and poor young men who have not interest here do not feel inclined to defend men and their property who will not defend themselvs, therefore we would ernestly solicit you to hasten us state protection before we are entirely broken up and ruined.

I now wish to bring before you, and to your immediate consideration facts poten[t] with meaning to us as a people, and for confermation of which you can find ample testimony, Robert Wolsey, a respectable citizen of our county has just reached home from Fort Arbuckle, while there the Comanche Cheif reached home for a visit to the camps of Those Indians who are now depredating upon us, they are camped some 3 or 4 hundred miles N.W. of Arbuckle on the Arkansas River, he says that the stock they have round them is immence stolen from this frontier, they have a depot of trade established with Kansas, they furnish them with arms and amunition etc getting their stock for little or nothing and still no doubt incouraging them to depradate upon us. Could not this thing be broken up by the President of the U.S. can you not bring these matters before him immediately for unless this trafic is broken up with Kansas we will always be troubled on this frontier. Mr Wolsey furthers States that the rade which carried off Boxs family had reached their camps and were proffering to return them to Texas or to a half way point some where, for their equivalent in Specie, for further proof of the locality of these savages and their carrying on trade with Kansas is veryfied in the case of a citizen of Jacksboro in Jack County who has just returned from their camp with a half dozen or more purchased captives, he penetrated to their camp from the state of Kansas, he says that they are well prepared for war and are very numerous, that no less than 15 hundred or 2 thousand men well armed would have any business of undertaking campeign in to their country for the purpos of putting an end to them, this ought to be done if it could be, for while they are allowed to remain in their present position and carry on a trade with the people of Kansas, our condition on this frontier will allways be a precarious one Gen. enquire farther into this matter and let the authoritys at Washington City be apprise of it at once.

With a cincere hope of Speedy relief and of better times yet to come I close by ascribing in myself Your

Obed Servt
W.H. Whaley

The following letters address the issue of kidnapping on the Texas frontier. During the nineteenth century, hundreds of white women and children were kidnapped from isolated settlements. They were often subjected to cruel treatment, and many lived for years with their captors. Often, negotiations to release the captives were tricky and fraught with danger.

Questions

1. Who was returning the captive? What consequences might he face for returning this boy?
2. Mark Walker expressed several concerns about the situation. What issues threatened the boy's safe return?
3. W. T. Sherman's reply to Walker was terse and merciless. What was Sherman's main priority? What did he demand?
4. Was there a possibility of the captive's safe return? Explain your answer.

Document 2

Mark Walker to Chauncy McKeever, May 14, 1867. Texas Indian Papers, Volume 4, #140, Archives and Information Services Division, Texas State Library and Archives Commission. Original in the Records in the Department of Interior, Office of Indian Affairs, Letters Received, Kiowa, 1867.[2]

Headquarters, Post of
Arbuckle, C.N.
May 14th 1867

Sir.
I have the honor to State that I have had an interview with To-ho-ye-qua-ih or Horse Back, of the Noconi band of Comanches (by means of the Interpreter.) He has in his possession a Captive White boy by the name of "Babb," thirteen years of age, Captured Septr. 1866, in Texas. The child was Stolen by the young men of Horse Backs tribe, and it has cost him considerable to get the child from its captors.

He proposes to give up the child, but is anxious to be renumerated for this trouble and expenses in obtaining it. Horse Backs professions of friendship are loud, and I believe him to be Sincere. I expla- a part of his duty to return the child, also to restrain his tribe from depredations and violence on the part of the whites; that I would write for instructions in the case, when he promised that he would take good care of the child, until he should here from me.

2 Copyright in the Public Domain.

The father of the child is a very poor
man and very Anxious that something
Should be done to restore it to him, as he is
fearful of its being Sold from tribe to tribe,
and finally lose it altogether

Very respectfully,
Your Obt Serv.
Mark Walker
1st Leuit, 19th crss [?] Infantry
Comdg Post.

Reports his interview
with To-ho-ye-qua-ih, or
Horse Back, of the Noco-
ni band of Comanches,
concerning the giving
up a white boy, named
"Babb," captured Septbr,
1866, in Texas.
++

Document 3

Headqrs. Mil: Dive: of the Mo. St Louis, Mo., June 19th, 1867[3]

Respectfully referred to Majr;
Genl. W.S. Hancock, Comdg Dept. of
the Mo. for his action in the case.
By order of Lieut Genl. Sherman.

W.A. Nichols
Assist Adgt Genl

3 Copyright in the Public Domain.

Hdqrs. Mil: Div. of the Mo,
Fort Leavenworth, Kan. Jun 25/67.
This paper happens to meet me here, It is now about as good a time as any for us to come to an understanding and rather than Submit to this practice of paying for Stolen children. It is better the Indian race be obliterated. I now have power to call out the volunteer force of the frontier, and the Commanding officer of Fort Arbuckle, may in his own way convey notice to the tribe that this boy must be Surrendered or else war to the death will be ordered.

There must be no ransom paid.
(Signed) W.T. Sherman
Lieut. Genl. Comdg.
++

Document 4

Headqrs. Dept of the Mo., Ft. Leavenworth, Kans., June 26th, 1867[4]

Respectfully referred to the Commanding officer, Dist. of the Indian Territory, inviting attention to the endorsement of the Lieut

4 Copyright in the Public Domain.

General Commanding, who will instruct the commanding officer of Fort Arbuckle to demand the Surrender of the Boy from Horse Backs Tribe, and without ransom.

By command of Major
Genl. Hancock;
Signed C. McKeever
Asst Adgt General

CPSIA information can be obtained
at www.ICGtesting.com
Printed in the USA
LVHW101224160720
660843LV00007B/198